WOMAN
you are
Called
& Anointed

GLENDA MALMIN

Published by City Bible Publishing
(Formerly Bible Temple Publishing)
9200 NE Fremont
Portland, Oregon 97220

Printed in U.S.A.

City Bible Publishing is a ministry of City Bible Church (formerly Bible Temple), and
is dedicated to serving the local church and its leaders through the production and
distribution of quality restoration materials.

It is our prayer that these materials, proven in the context of the local church, will
equip leaders in exalting the Lord and extending His kingdom.

For a free catalog of additional resources from City Bible Publishing please call
1-800-777-6057 or visit our web site at www.citybiblepublishing.com.

I would like to dedicate this book to my daughter, Angela, and my daughter-in-law, Rebecca, two incredibly anointed young women who are serving the Lord and His people with all of their hearts. May you both continue to walk fearlessly in the grace and anointing with which the Lord Jesus has called you.

I would also like to dedicate this book to all the young women who are seeking the knowledge of the will of God for their lives and are bravely stepping into His service. "He who calls you is faithful, who also will do it" (I Thessalonians 5:24). Enjoy the journey!

Acknowledgements

I give honor and thanks to the Lord Jesus for giving me salvation as a precious and personal gift. I am forever grateful for the call and everything that it entails. Thank you for allowing me to walk with my hand in Yours.

I would like to thank my husband, Ken, for his many years of faithfulness, encouragement and inspiration. It is a joy to walk together in the journey to which the Lord has called us. Thank you for releasing me to be all that God has called me to be.

I would also like to thank my personal prayer partners, Donna, Linda, Darla, Kelly, Detta, Susan, Melody, Andrea, Fred, Lynn, Robert and Donna. You are indeed testimonies of the power of partnership in the Kingdom of God. It is a blessing to never have to walk alone in the service of our King. I pray that this book will honor the hours of prayer that you have put into it.

TABLE OF CONTENTS

Foreword

Preface: I Am Willing Lord-Aren't I?

Foreword

❋

We are very excited about *Woman You Are Called and Anointed!* Glenda has taught the practical and spiritual insights in this book for years with enthusiastic reception, and women have been changed for life as a result. Her desire is to see women, especially young women, fulfill their calling in the Body of Christ and reach their full potential for the establishment of the Kingdom of God.

We have known Glenda and her husband, Ken, for 28 years, and our respect for them has only grown over the years. Glenda is the Dean of Women at Portland Bible College, which is affiliated with City Bible Church, and Ken is one of the Executive Pastors at the church and also functions as the Dean of the college. Both of them have taught there for over 20 years with godly wisdom and have successful fruit all over the world.

Glenda has functioned and continues to function in a variety of roles: wife, mother, counselor, retreat and seminar speaker, Bible college teacher and currently Dean of Women. She continues to be a godly example of a woman who has developed her God-given gifts and talents along with her focus on the importance of having a Christ-like character.

Woman You are Called and Anointed will challenge women on the journey of Christ-like servanthood and leadership as they fulfill their God given calling. Women having any level of spiritual responsibility will also be equally encouraged.

Pastors Frank & Sharon Damazio
City Bible Church
Portland, Oregon

PREFACE
I Am Willing Lord–Aren't I?

Although I have been in some form of Christian leadership for many years now, this book is not just written for pastors' wives or Christian women who are functioning in areas of public ministry. It is written for all women who have ever wondered about the personal calling of God. It is written for women who are willing to hear the calling of God and to do something about what they hear.

Over the years I have spoken with numerous young women who say they feel "called." They feel "called" to be women of God, or "called" to make a difference, or "called" to be a pastor's wife. Upon hearing this, I have often wondered what kind of picture comes to mind when this profession of "calling" is made.

You probably would not have picked up this book if you hadn't had some thought or question in regard to your calling as a believer in Jesus Christ. Perhaps you are reading this because you have felt "the call." You earnestly desire to be an influential woman for Christ. You are eager, ready and willing. You are simply waiting for the Lord to give you marching orders. Your cry is "I am willing, Lord!"

Perhaps you picked up this book because you are in a position of influence in the Kingdom of God, but you are tired, weary and ready to quit. You have found that the call to model Christ is more challenging than you have ever imagined. You have wondered why no one ever told you the full price of "the call." Sometimes you have even found yourself wishing you had never heard "the call." Your cry is "I am willing, Lord–aren't I?"

If you are a minister's wife, you may have found yourself trying to decipher between your call and that of your husband. You may have found that "the calling" of "two being one" requires more than you have ever imagined it would. At times, you have found yourself proclaiming, "I am willing, Lord!" and, at other times, adding faintly, "aren't I?"

Whatever your station or season in life, I pray that the pastor of your heart, the Good Shepherd, will renew your spirit and encourage your steps as you read these pages. I pray that you will feel His grace shower down on you like a warm, spring rain.

Whether you are reading this because you are attempting to discern His calling or are simply in need of a fresh touch of enabling anointing, know that the place of discernment and refreshing still lies at the feet of Jesus. It is at His feet that you will not only hear His voice, but will also receive His anointing to do the task that He sets before you.

Personal calling is not something that can be written in a book or schemed up in your mind. It is something that is very personal and uniquely ordained for you by God. It always involves other people, and it is usually much simpler than your own plans and designs. To hear God's call and walk in His anointing, you must live close to the hearts of people and within the hearing of His voice. To keep this divine balance you must stay ever close to Him in the journey.

To be called by God and anointed to serve Him and the people for whom He died is a tremendous privilege and high calling. Jesus said, "My yoke is easy and my burden is light" (Matthew 11:20). Woman, you are called and anointed.

SECTION ONE:

your
Call

Chapter 1

THE CALL
Who God Has Called You to Be

The speaker had concluded his evening message by saying, "Take your candle, walk across the field and talk to God. Oh yes, stay at least fifteen feet away from anyone else."

It was the last night of youth camp and I was fifteen years old. The distractions were many and the emotions were varied. "How would I say goodbye to this new boy who had just walked into my life this week? Then again, he wasn't as cute as my friend's new boyfriend, so maybe it wouldn't be so hard after all. How romantic to be sent out into a starlit field in the evening with only a small candle in hand. What did the speaker say–talk to God? Well, I know how to pray at bedtime and at the dinner table, but what would I do out there with God and my candle for a whole twenty minutes?"

That's how "the call" began for me. How did it begin for you? Today spending twenty minutes with God is less than opening comments in my conversations with Him. But when I was fifteen, although I had experienced His sovereignty in my life, I hadn't known how to experience His personal closeness until this youth camp experience. It was when I took that walk into the starlit field that evening that I not only talked to

God, He talked to me. He called to me personally and placed certain aspirations and goals in my heart for my future with Him.

It's a great day to be a woman who personally knows and walks with her God. It's a day when God is openly and specifically calling many. To respond to His call is challenging, fun and heart-expanding.

Although the call is free, it's costly. It will stretch you beyond your personal capabilities and creative senses yet bless you more than you can imagine. It will take you places that you never imagined you could go, and it will hold you in places that you will at times long to break free of. It will require of you a sensitive ear, courageous heart and closer walk.

From the genesis of creation to the end of the age, God has always been and will always be innovative and personally caring in the calling of His people. He is a very creative and personal God, and thus deals with His people in such manner.

I don't know about you, but sometimes I seem to lack the creative discernment and ability to keep up with Him. I seem to lack the ability to hear His voice accurately. Sometimes, in my dullness of mind, I have foolishly charged Him with lack of awareness and care, only to realize later that I was the one lacking in vision and creative response. At times like these, I say, "I am willing Lord, aren't I?"

Only recently, God and I were having this kind of conversation. I was complaining that He had not moved in my life or in my circumstance the way that I thought He should. I felt that He was not keeping up His end of the bargain appropriately. It seemed that He was not fulfilling His calling in my life. Circumstances were not lining up in the way I thought they should; at least, not when I compared my life to the lives of my peers.

In the midst of my complaint, I couldn't discern His specific and unique guidance. I misinterpreted direction that I felt had been very specific and clear in the past. Unwise comparison had dulled my ears to the sound of God's unique calling for me. I began to wonder if His real "calling" was only for a specific few.

As I humbled myself before Him, much against my carnal will, I caught a glimpse of His unique pathway for me. Although His initial calling had within it a similar melody and structure to that of my peers, it had its own unique variations that were composed specifically for me.

As I write this, tears stream down my face at the realization of my great lack and His great love. To realize how creative and specific is the calling, placement, and anointing of God, is to realize how personal and intimate is His love. How wise was the Psalmist when he said to the Lord, "My times are in Your hand . . ." (Psalm 31:15).

What Is the Call?

Jesus says in Matthew 9:37-38, "The harvest is so great, and the workers are so few. So pray to the one in charge of harvesting, ask him to recruit more workers for his harvest fields" (Living).

Herein lies the call. Are you willing to be called as an individual daughter? Truly the harvest is great, and the laborers are so very few. If you are presently involved in ministering to others, you know that truth already. You should never hide behind a title or stereotype. Rather, simply do that which He has called you to do as His disciple.

The statistics of alcoholism, abuse of every sort, abortion, out-of-wedlock pregnancies, divorce, murder, rape and a variety of other wounds in every nation around the world ring out with the need for the message of Christ. There is a tremendous need for more workers. Hosea 4:6 says, "My people are destroyed [dumb, silent] for lack of knowledge. . . ."

It's time to stand a little taller, bend the knee a little lower, listen closely and, then, do and say whatever the Lord tells you to do and say. It's time to "break through" the silence and the destruction and release the knowledge of the Lord Jesus Christ to this generation.

Whether that "breaking through" comes in the form of hospitality, teaching, color coordinating, home schooling, singing special solos, becoming the best employee or supervisor at work or a variety of other things, you must be absolutely faithful to do whatever it is that God has called you to do, not because of whose wife or whose employee you are, but because of Whose daughter you are.

Your life will not be made fruitful by simply dreaming dreams. It will be made fruitful by the choices you make and act upon. Take this moment to reflect on your own heart motivations. Simply ask the Lord to touch you and renew your willingness to be exactly who He wants you to be. The "doing" in your life will come and go in seasons of time, however the "being" must remain constant. If you are being who God wants you to be, then you'll be on target in the doing.

Is Everyone Called?

Have you ever wondered if the calling and anointing of God is only for a few? Is it only offered to those who have a long-standing, Christian family heritage? Is it only for those with certain personalities, talents and social status? Does it depend on marital status or gender?

The Bible clearly addresses these questions with both verve and tenderness. For example, in the first chapter of Galatians, Paul tells us that God separated him from his mother's womb and called him through His grace. In Ephesians, Paul tells the Gentiles that with their acceptance of Christ comes the calling of God. In I Corinthians, he tells us that it's not necessarily the smartest or the strongest whom God calls, but rather those who recognize their need to depend on Him. Peter tells servants, in I Peter chapter one, that they are called and that the suffering-Christ left His example for them. John, the beloved disciple of Jesus, bursts on the scene in chapter three of I John and says, "Behold what manner of love the Father has bestowed on us, that we should be called children of God! . . ."

The entire New Testament exhorts that no matter what our lineage, talents, gender, social or marital status, once we have accepted Christ as our personal Savior, there is a calling to which each of us must personally respond. With that calling comes an enabling anointing to carry out the call.

The Old Testament is also rich with admonition through the lives of both men and women in a variety of vocations, social stations and marital situations. Each person, who heard the call of God and responded, had a unique part to play in history.

The God, who called Eve, Sarah, Rebekah, Naomi, Rahab, Mary and all the rest in ancient history, is the same God who calls us today. Their very examples tell us that His calling is not only for a few. It is not only for those with a special lineage, talent, gender or social status. Again, we see that His call is to all who will respond, and with that calling comes the grace and anointing to fulfill it.

Whether you are single, married, rich, poor, a full-time homemaker, career woman or somewhere in between, there is a call from the Lord for you. Whether you think you are qualified or disqualified by your moral past, whether you have several college degrees or none, the future is bright under the canopy of His anointing. The Lord is calling at the doorstep of your heart, and His enabling anointing is only a step of faith away.

Is This My Husband's Call or Mine?

If you are a pastor's wife or want to be a pastor's wife, I have to tell you honestly at the outset of this book, I do not believe God calls women to be "pastors' wives." I believe that He calls each individual woman to minister uniquely. If you are married to a pastor, lay-minister, reverend or priest, then you are a "pastor's wife," and that combined role will have some unique responsibilities and privileges. However, I am not so sure that God calls women specifically to be "pastors' wives" any more than He calls women to be doctors' wives, politicians' wives, or astronauts' wives.

In marriage, the husband's vocation will have as much effect on the wife's role as her vocation may have on his. However, each member of the marriage union, husband and wife, is personally called by the Lord.

Perhaps this point seems like mere semantics. However, I believe that members of the Body of Christ have been genuinely hurt, having been coerced or pressured into living out stereotypes that God has neither defined nor ordained in Scripture. If you are a pastor's wife who feels uncomfortably molded by a predisposed stereotype, Christ wants to break the mold. He wants to release you to be all that He has called you to be, personally, as a wife and as a Christian woman of influence.

Personally functioning with the gifts and talents that God has given to each of us will free those around us to function in their gifts and talents. This releases single women from needing to search for a marriage partner in order to gain falsely assumed credibility. It also releases wives from being dependent on their husbands' callings.

I have seen many godly, married women sit and wait for their destinies to be fulfilled by their husbands' callings or job descriptions. Sadly, as this waiting takes place, many precious opportunities to share the love of Christ become missed opportunities.

The question I would like to present is this: "What are women waiting for?" Whether you are married or unmarried, allow me to personalize this and ask, "Are you waiting for someone else's title to define your calling? Are you waiting to be a pastor's wife, a doctor's wife, a boss's secretary or a president's vice president?"

I am not minimizing the importance of the wife's role or of being in a supportive role in a job or ministry function. However, surely there is something broader and more personal to your calling than one role! If you're married, being a wife may be one facet of your calling, but it is not meant to be all encompassing. Married or unmarried, if you're functioning in a supportive role in any job or ministry, that is also only one facet of the person that God has called you to be.

God cares about you personally and, therefore, calls you personally. He does not define you by another person's call. Again, using the marriage analogy, if your call is merely to be someone's wife, then you must ask, what happens to your call if your husband dies or decides to leave his position? If your calling was only to be someone's wife and your husband died, then your call would die with him. However, if you have a personal calling and your husband leaves his position, your job description may change, but the calling will not. You will simply rediscover your calling in the context of a new job description.

I observed this first hand with my prior senior pastor's wife, Edie. She and her husband, Dick Iverson, were my pastors for over twenty-seven years. They pastored our church for over forty years. In the early years of Edie's ministry, she served closely alongside her husband and aided him in making the primary decisions of the church and in leading the church services on Sunday mornings. Although she was still a primary influence in the decision making process, as the church grew and other leaders were added to the team, Edie was released to focus her energy and vision in another direction and became the head of the children's and women's ministries. Now that she and her husband have relinquished their primary pastoral role in the church, she is currently traveling with him and advising other pastors' wives.

Regardless of the season that Edie has found herself in, she has always functioned in the gifts that God has personally given to her. She has never tried to fit into someone else's predisposed stereotype of what a pastor's wife should be; she has always functioned vibrantly in her own personal gifts and talents. In doing so, she has released many women around her to be all that God has called them to be. I truly honor her as a gift to the Body of Christ.

Whether you're a wife or not, the principal of personal calling relates to you. Every Christian woman needs to function uniquely according to her individual calling. Each is a "daughter of the King," who is called to impart to this generation the deposit Christ has given her (Psalm 45:13). That calling is not dependent upon another's calling. It may complement and be complemented by another's calling, but it is an individual calling that stands in its own right. This is true for every individual woman.

Am I Called in This Season of Life?

When I was younger, Edie Iverson once said to me, "If you're young, don't try to be old." In other words, be who you are in whatever season of life you are. Perhaps you're young and long to be older and wiser; perhaps you're older and wiser but long to be younger and more energetic. We need to always be who we are, wherever the Lord has placed us. To do this is to walk in His calling.

Henry Ford II was once noted as saying, "A company needs to be constantly rejuvenated by the influx of young blood. It needs smart young men with the imagination and guts to turn everything upside down if they can. It also needs old fogies to keep them from turning upside down those things that ought to be right side up. Above all, it needs young rebels and old conservatives who can work together, challenge each other's views, yield or hold fast with equal grace, and continue after each hard-fought battle to respect each other as men and as colleagues."

Now, from a Christian perspective, we may not agree with some of Henry Ford's terminology, but his point is well taken. The Christian community needs people from a variety of ages, personalities, shapes and sizes. If there ceases to be diversity within the Body of Christ, how will we reach the variety of people outside the church walls who do not know Christ?

I love the way Paul says it in I Timothy 4:11-16, "Get the word out. Teach all these things. And don't let anyone put you down because you're young. Teach believers with your life: by word, by demeanor, by love, by faith, by integrity. Stay at your post reading Scripture, giving counsel, teaching. And that special gift of ministry you were given when the leaders of the church laid hands on you and prayed–keep that dusted off and in use. Cultivate these things. Immerse yourself in them. The people will all see you mature right before their eyes! Keep a firm grasp on both your character and your teaching. Don't be diverted. Just keep at it. Both you and those who hear you will experience salvation" (The Message).

Jeremiah of the Old Testament was just a young teenager when God called him to be a prophet to the nation. Jeremiah felt a bit hesitant about that calling because of his age. Jeremiah 1:7-9 says, "But the Lord said to me: 'Do not say, "I am a child," for you shall go to all to whom I send you, and whatever I command you, you shall speak. Do not be afraid of their faces, for I am with you to deliver you,' says the Lord. Then the Lord put forth His hand and touched my mouth, and the Lord said to me: 'Behold, I have put My words in your mouth.' "

When the Lord says to you, as He did to Jeremiah, "Therefore prepare yourself and arise, and speak to them all that I command you," call out as Jeremiah did. Say, "I see a branch of an almond tree" (Jeremiah 1:11). The almond tree represented fruitfulness to Jeremiah, so when he said this, he was really saying, "I see proof that fruit is about to bud." After this statement of revelation and faith, the Lord said to Jeremiah, "You have seen well, for I am ready to perform My word" (Jeremiah 1:12).

Jeremiah refused to look to his excuses of youthfulness and inexperience. Instead he looked to the call of God and to the fruit that would come through His obedience to the call. Look afresh and see clearly what the Master sees.

Since Christ accepts you just as you are in this moment, you should also accept yourself and your season of life, as Jeremiah did. The shortest portion of your life will be spent here on earth, so be quick to follow the Lord's leading and enjoy serving Him in whatever season you are in. Remember that job descriptions may vary through the years, but the personal calling of the Master will ring true to your heart in each season.

Notice that Jeremiah didn't argue with the Lord over his season in life. He shared his surprise and then accepted the Lord's perspective. When he did this the Lord "touched his mouth." God touched his ability to speak, and anointed him to do that which He called him to do.

Can't Someone Else Do It?

Never attempt to give your calling to someone else; no one else can fulfill it. Others may have job descriptions from the Lord that look the same as yours, but they are not the same. Have confidence that God will anoint whatever and whomever He has called. You simply need to be responsive and obedient to His call. I Thessalonians 5:24 says, "Faithful is He who calls you who also will do it."

You may be saying to yourself at this point, "It would be easier to just sit in the church pew once a week. Do I really have to do something about this personal tugging that I feel so deeply in my heart? I feel stirred, but afraid and definitely inadequate." What is that call that is stirring within you? The true call is to be just exactly what God has called you to be—nothing more and nothing less. You can do that. Regardless of the season or the place to which He has called you, you can do that.

In Matthew 25:14-30, the Parable of the Talents, the Lord shows that He has given each of us certain talents. In this parable, He holds each of us responsible only for what He has given to us individually. He does not hold us responsible for what He has given to someone else.

You are unique. No one else in history is exactly like you. Not one other person has exactly the same combination of talents, gifts, personality, family placement, heritage and calling that you have. The good news is that you're required by God to invest only the talents that He has given to you. You are required, however, to develop what He has given you to its fullest potential.

He may have gifted you to be a politician, a cosmetologist, a teacher or a doctor. He may have put administration, counseling or care-taking skills within your mind and heart. Whatever talent He has invested in you, that is what He expects you to develop. No one else can do what you are called to do in exactly the same way that you would do it.

Sarai of the Old Testament tried that once (see Genesis 12-16). God told Abram and Sarai in Genesis 12:2-3, " . . . I will make you a great nation; I will bless you and make your name great; and you shall be a blessing. . . . And in you all the families of the earth shall be blessed."

Sarai got tired of waiting for the fulfillment of this promise. She couldn't see it happening, nor did she have the confidence for it any longer. She was weary of waiting for the release of the promise, so she decided to try to give away her call. She took notice of her maidservant, Hagar, who was looking like she could very well fulfill what God had called Sarai to do. Then she manipulated Abram, her husband, until he agreed to her plot. She tried to take the pressure off of herself to fulfill the Word of the Lord.

Can you relate to that?! Have you ever caught yourself thinking, "I am tired of waiting around for this to be fulfilled. There goes a willing soul. I'll just let her do it!"

Sarai's life teaches us to never manipulate innocent, willing servants, or those who love us, into fulfilling what we ourselves have been called to do! The very best that Hagar, the Egyptian maid, could have done was to give birth to her son, Ishmael, not Isaac. She could not have produced Isaac even if her greatest heart's desire was to please Sarai. That was Sarai's call, not hers.

After Hagar conceived the seed, she began to despise Sarai. She began to cling with a motherly affection to her son. Sarai saw this and then charged Abram with the wrong. Abram, in frustration as well as utter love for Sarai, told her to do with Hagar as she wished.

What happens today to innocent co-workers, Bible study buddies or loving husbands when women try to give away their callings? Do they become despised and despise in return—for the sake of the call? Do they cause unnecessary frustration to those who love them? Is birth given to "Ishmael" ministries, programs and plans that perhaps should never have been? Does "Isaac" still remain unbirthed? Christian women everywhere must be willing to discern and yield to the call, and then wait on its fulfillment.

Several years ago, a young, single adult, whom my husband and I knew, lost his life in a tragic accident. He was the only son in his family. At his funeral service, his father said to my husband, "I guess I will have to do the ministry that God called me to do long ago. I always felt that my son would fulfill that calling, but I guess I must do it now." Whether that son would have gone into the ministry and done a great work for God or not, he still would not have fulfilled what God had asked his father to do.

No one else can do what you have been called to do, not one who is more gifted or one who is more naturally talented. It must be you.

Can Anyone Hinder the Fulfillment of My Call?

I once attended a women's conference in Chicago, and the title of one teaching session was "God Has Anointed You—Now Deal With It." What a great thought! God has called you; He has anointed you. Now "deal with it." In other words, He has done His part; now you do yours.

No one can keep you from fulfilling the call of God on your life—except you. Although God may define your calling with a different title than you anticipated, if you look closely, it will still be your calling.

All too often, potentially influential Christian women are hindered in their God-ordained callings by their own responses to other peoples' perceptions of what women should and shouldn't do. Some may feel hindered by their seasons of life, others by role definitions. Neither should hinder you from fulfilling the call of God on your life.

Perhaps God called you to preach the gospel. When you heard the call, you immediately interpreted it as meaning to preach to large crowds of adults today–not tomorrow, but today. You look and discover that you are preaching to four-year-olds on Sunday mornings. If this fits you somewhat and you are feeling hemmed in by this group of small-sized disciples, let the life of Henrietta Mears, founder of Gospel Light Publications, expand your vision and definition of calling.

Henrietta is considered one of the most influential women in the mid-twentieth century Church. She was a high school chemistry teacher in Minneapolis in the 1920s. During this time, at the request of her pastor, she accepted the challenge of teaching a Sunday school class of five, eighteen-year-old girls. As she faithfully taught those five girls, the class grew to over five hundred in attendance. The church had to build a special hall to accommodate them.

In 1928, she became the Director of Christian Education at another church and then became involved in full-time Christian ministry. When she began her ministry there, the children's Sunday school enrollment was four hundred fifty. In two and a half years, that number increased to more than four thousand.

Soon after she began her ministry in this location, she developed her own Sunday school curriculum. Within just a few short years, orders for her Sunday school lessons were coming in from all over the nation. This was the beginning of Gospel Light Publications.

Besides Henrietta's writing and publishing ministry, she is particularly well known for her teaching of young men. Among her students were Bill Bright, the founder of Campus Crusade for Christ, Richard Halverson, pastor of the Presbyterian Church in Washington, DC, and Harold Ockenga, a noted evangelical leader in Boston.

The late Clarence Roddy, professor of homiletics at Fuller Seminary, used to refer to Miss Mears as "the best preacher in Southern California." He said, "She was not ordained and had no formal theological training, but the impact of her life and teaching on her boys was comparable to the influence some of the world's greatest theologians had on their students."

Henrietta's life beautifully teaches that if you are truly called by God, no one but you can stop that calling. In this moment, yield your yearnings and logical reasoning to God. You are called. Now deal with it, yield to it and let God define it.

How Will I Respond?

Are you willing to be recruited by the Master? He wants to recruit you to do nothing more and nothing less–only what He has asked you to do. Let me add that you do not need to go into a paid ministry position to do a great work for God. We are all called to be His able ministers.

John Wesley, a great man in church history, is known for saying, "Give me a hundred men who fear nothing but sin, and desire nothing but God, and I will shake the world. I care not a straw whether they be clergymen or laymen; and such alone will overthrow the kingdom of Satan and build up the Kingdom of God on earth."

This is a great statement in and of itself. However, allow me to rephrase it this way: "Lord, call a hundred men and women, who care not a straw about their gender or position in regard to Your calling, who will fear nothing but sin, and desire nothing but You alone. Take them and shake the world with their unity under Your lordship. Such alone will overthrow the kingdom of Satan and build up the Kingdom of God on earth."

Be the woman who Jesus has anointed you to be, and do what He has called you to do. His timing and placement have been with much forethought and planning. Graciously respond to His placement and His plan. This is clearly a day when God is calling openly and specifically to many women. He desires to empower us with His anointing to fulfill that which He calls us to do.

Chapter 2

INFLUENCE

An Example of the Believer

When I was in my first year of college, the clarion call to every young woman who really wanted to do something with her life was to "make a mark" and "make a difference" for women in our generation. The possibilities were not only endless, but fascinating as well. The presented challenge was both bold and exciting. However, there were a few things they never told us about being women of influence. There were a few price tags left unmarked.

I had certainly tried to prepare myself for this challenge by enrolling only in "college prep" courses in high school and by doing my best to avoid any classes that hinted of the female domestics from the previous generation. (That, by the way, is much to my regret today.) I was exhilarated by the thought of the opportunities ahead of me.

As I sat in my freshman college classes, there was one particular faculty member who inspired me. Not only was the instructor capable of captivating my interest in a subject that I cared little about, but she was also a "real" woman, by my estimation. She was intelligent, respected by her male peers, yet very feminine. I was somewhat in awe and chose to yield myself to her influence. I thought to myself, "Now here is a woman who I would like to model myself after."

Then one day during a class session, she made this comment to the class: "The time has come. You must cut the umbilical cord between yourself and your parents." Although I realized that every young adult needed to emotionally separate from his or her parents, assume adult responsibilities, and become a responsible citizen in his or her own rite, I also realized that her statement had a deeper insinuation. My mind began to reel as she continued to emphasize her point. I looked around the class and everyone seemed to be absorbing what she said as though it were some form of newly enlightened truth.

As for me, I not only respected my parents; I actually liked them. An emotional struggle began within me between my newly discovered role model and my ever-faithful role models at home. I decided upon the "ever-faithful." They had a good track record with me, and there was something disconcerting about the statement of my newly discovered role model and the spirit in which she said it. It seemed extreme and risky. Although my spiritual discernment was not very sharp at that time, her words no longer bore witness with my spirit. I respected her as an instructor, but no longer as a mentor.

Am I to Be an Example?

As was true of my generation, young women today are also crying out for mentors and those who are willing to disciple them. They are looking for those who believe in them and are willing to lead them into something exciting, meaningful and fruitful. They are not easily duped by feminist jargon. However, they are vulnerable to those who are willing to invest time and energy in them personally.

Young women today are looking for mentors who are willing to be transparent and are actually modeling something worth following. They want example, but they also want reality. As followers of Christ, we should be the examples.

Whether you are working as an architect, a waitress or a computer technologist, if you are a Christian, you are called to be an example. Whether you live in a rural neighborhood or an urban high-rise complex, if you are a Christian, you are called to be an example. Whether you are single, married, divorced or widowed, if you are a Christian, you are called to be an example.

Sometimes when a woman initially hears the call, she fails to hear the definition behind the call. She hears, "preach, teach, heal, etc.," but her ears don't pick up on the principles of "leading by example," "bearing your cross" or "others may, but you may not."

Some women dream of hearing people say, "I want to be just like her." Instead they hear criticisms of their hair or their newest pair of shoes. They imagine people being astounded by their insight into Scripture. Instead they receive comments on their need for grammar improvement. They imagine people being impressed with their singing skills. Instead the name of "a really good voice teacher" is proffered. Can you relate to any of this?

Actually, numerous times I have imagined myself falling flat on my face as I descend the stairs from the platform in our church. Of course, this always follows a "not so profound" statement I have just made. Now that would be quite an example, wouldn't it?! It would be entertaining, yes–edifying, no. What kind of role model have you imagined yourself to be?

What Does the Bible Say About Being an Example?

One little word is repeated several times in Scripture with the call to minister and be a strong Christian witness to others. That word is "example" (some translations say "imitate"). This little word will add color and definition to your calling as a Christian woman of influence. This little word also has a personal price tag attached to it. It will sometimes make you uncomfortable when everyone else in the room is comfortable and peaceful when everyone else is in distress. This little word will also compel you to trust in Jesus completely as you become aware of the many eyes that are on you. Simply said, this little word is what this generation is looking for.

Take just a moment to read the following few verses; please don't just skim over them, but really think about them. In reality, nothing that I say in these pages has the power to affect you for very long, but meditating on these Scriptures can engrave a message into your heart that will keep you on "the straight and narrow" up to the time that you will cross over into eternity.

"Therefore, I urge you to *imitate me*" (I Corinthians 4:16, NIV).

"Remember those who led you, who spoke the word of God to you; and considering the outcome of their way of life, *imitate their faith*" (Hebrews 13:7, NAS).

"You, however, *know all about* my teaching, *my way of life*, my purpose, faith, patience, love, endurance . . ." (II Timothy 3:10, NIV).

"For our gospel did not come to you in word only, but also in power and in the Holy Spirit and with full conviction; just as you know what kind of men we proved to be among you for your sake. You also became *imitators of us* and of the Lord, having received the word in much tribulation with the joy of the Holy Spirit" (I Thessalonians 1:5-6, NAS).

"For you yourselves know how you ought to follow *our example*, because we did not act in an undisciplined manner among you" (II Thessalonians 3:7, NAS).

"Brethren, join in *following my example*, and observe those who walk according to the pattern you have in us" (Philippians 3:17, NAS).

"*Follow my example* as I follow the example of Christ" (I Corinthians 11:1, NIV).

"In everything *set them an example* by doing what is good . . . so that those who oppose you may be ashamed because they have nothing bad to say" (Titus 2:7-8, NIV).

"Let no one despise your youth, but *be an example* to the believers in word, in conversation, in charity, in spirit, in faith, in purity" (I Timothy 4:12).

These Scriptures, if read with an understanding heart, will shake you to the core of your spirit and keep you utterly dependent not on "the call," but on God Himself. Every time I read these Scriptures, I feel the need to walk very close to the Master. I know that within myself there is all too often weakness where there should be strength, anxiousness where there should be peace and frustration where there should be compassion. Sadly, too often there is also coolness where there should be warmth, distrust where there should be trust, discipline where there should be grace, and grace where there should be more discipline. I sometimes laugh when I should cry and cry when I should be full of faith.

My list could go on. I am sure you could also write a list of reasons why you are hesitant to encourage people to imitate you and to follow your example and your way of life, as Paul so often said.

Encouragement is found in what Paul also said in I Timothy 1:15: "This is a faithful saying and worthy of all acceptance, that Christ Jesus came into the world to save sinners, of whom I am chief." Not only does Paul say that he identifies with our weaknesses as a "chief" sinner, but He also reminds us that it is Christ Jesus who saves the lost, not us. Even though the command rings out loudly that we are to be willing examples to those around us, it is only our example as we follow Christ that is emphasized. It is the "Christ in you that is the hope of glory" (Colossians1:27). It is with courage and dependence on Christ that we are enabled to lead by example.

Our example is to flow out of a deep awareness of our dependence on His grace. It is out of that awareness that grace should flow to others as well. One of your primary goals should be to be a dispenser of His grace. To be a true example of the believer in every facet is to model the love and grace of our Lord Jesus Christ to those who are following.

I Timothy 4:12 gives us a very special key to this area of being an example. In the original King James translation, Paul tells young Timothy, his disciple, "be thou an example of the believer." He graciously does not say to be an example "to" the believer, but rather "of" the believer. How encouraging!

We all know that different people put different expectations on Christian believers. What one feels is appropriate, another would judge as inappropriate. What one would say is offensive, another would find refreshingly creative. I am thankful that I am not responsible to meet every person's individual expectations. Rather, I am only responsible to model what a Christian believer is to be according to God's Word, and I am to be measured by His grace level, not anyone else's. I find that not only accomplishable, but refreshing as well.

How Am I to Be an Example?

As women desiring to be positive influences, we are not called to be any more exemplary than any other believer is. So whether you are an ordained minister or not, if you are a disciple, you must be willing to be an example.

In this passage in Timothy, Paul gives his disciple six areas in which he is to be an example: "in word, in conduct, in love, in spirit, in faith, in purity." Let us take a closer look at these words.

In Word

I Timothy 4:12 says that we are to be exemplary "in word." In "word" not only means something spoken, but also includes the thought that was prior to the "word." More specifically, we are not to be gossips or loose-tongued.

A slogan during World War II was "loose lips sink ships." I have seen more than one church lose its life and reputation due to "loose lips." Christian men and women who speak out inappropriately on issues can do severe damage to the church and to the Lord's testimony in a community.

Proverbs 21:23 says, "Whoever guards his mouth and tongue, keeps his soul from troubles." Proverbs 4:23 charges, "Keep your heart with all diligence. For out of it spring the issues of life." Romans 12:3 says, "For I say, through the grace given to me, to everyone who is among you, not to think of himself more highly than he ought to think, but to think soberly, as God has dealt to each one a measure of faith." To "think soberly" in this passage, means to think with controlled thought, not to think in extremes.

All too often our unwisely spoken words come out of an unguarded heart and mind. As a Christian woman you must be careful not to let frayed hormones, personal insecurities, disappointments or frustrations dictate what comes out of your mouth.

The Psalmist has the right idea when he prays, "Set a guard, O Lord, over my mouth; keep watch over the door of my lips" (Psalm 141:3). This should be a constant prayer of every believer. Anytime we enter a room "mouth first" instead of mind and spirit first, we enter at great risk. The very way in which the Master designed us physically should communicate something to us of His intent in this area. Notice the two ears and the one mouth. This is probably God's indication that we should listen more than we speak. It is funny how easily we miss the obvious, isn't it? God instructs and guides us in such simple fashion that we often miss it.

Matthew 12:35-37 says, "A good man out of the good treasure of the heart brings forth good things, and an evil man out of the evil treasure brings forth evil things. But I say to you that for every idle word men may speak, they will give account of it in the day of judgment. For by your words you will be justified and by your words you will be condemned." Pray that the Lord will help you to bring good treasure out of your heart and out of your mouth. If you do this, not only will the praise of others come to you, but you will find that many will want to follow your example as well.

A woman who chooses her words wisely is a blessing not only to those around her, but also to other team members with whom she may work. I have never met a woman who constantly chatters or speaks thoughtlessly who also has the deep respect of both male and female co-workers. When a woman babbles like a brook, many men will evaluate her as frivolous in thought, foolish in speech or lacking in wisdom. When working with men, one must learn how to speak wisely, thoughtfully and with a few well-chosen words. Men generally do not have a great need for many adverbs and adjectives in order to understand the necessary facts of a situation. Colorful adjectives are fun and add to dialogue, but they are not always taken very seriously.

Think and pray before you speak. Again, never enter a room "mouth first." A woman of good judgment will choose her words wisely and speak them succinctly.

In Conduct

I Timothy 4:12 goes on to tell us that we should be an example in our conduct, as well as in our speech.

Being an example in conduct sometimes infers the concept "others may, but you may not." When you are called to a position of Christian influence, you give up your right to say and do whatever you want to at any time and in any way.

This is not to expunge from the mentor the message of grace that the Bible so clearly outlines. We are to be recipients of grace, as well as givers of grace. We are, in fact, to walk freely in the grace and liberty of the Lord. However, within the realms of grace, there is sometimes a price to be paid for the sake of influence. You may have to sacrifice some of your own liberties for the sake of on-looking unbelievers or other more spiritually fragile brothers and sisters in Christ.

Another way of saying this is that you must follow the commission that Jesus gave to His followers in Luke 9:23: ". . . If anyone desires to come after Me, let him deny himself, and take up his cross daily, and follow Me." Allow me to break this up into three challenges.

Let Him Deny Himself

To "deny yourself" simply means not to let your own personal happiness be the primary goal of your daily life. You must deal with your own self-centeredness. If you don't, how will you be able to effectively help others deal with theirs? People will not receive instruction or counsel from someone who lacks humility, is ignorant or is presently guilty of some issue that is, from their perspectives, worse than their own.

For example, if you work in an office and join in on the coffee break gossip, it will be hard for people to offer you their personal prayer requests after office hours. If you rule over people in a prideful manner instead of compassionately offering to help them in a time of need, it will be difficult for them to be motivated to follow the Christ you serve.

In the process of actively following Jesus daily, there will be numerous opportunities to deny your self-centered tendencies. For example, it is not uncommon for a woman, who is focused on ministering to the needs of others, to find herself taking a counseling class at the nearby local college instead of a preferred painting class, or taking an all-day computer class instead of going shopping. She may find herself organizing a funeral dinner instead of playing tennis with a friend, or visiting a new mother in the hospital while her children are left with the baby-sitter. The list is endless. You have probably been there more times than you want to remember.

Jesus kindly says that if you are really going to follow Him, you must be willing to deny yourself for the sake of others. You will never be able to ask others to sacrifice for the sake of Christ if they see you living a self-serving lifestyle.

Denial, however, does not mean despair. As you focus on the needs of others, Christ will actually pour blessings into your life. There will be times when you'll go shopping while others clean up after a wedding reception, or you'll have time to sit in the park and soak in the sunshine while others are called to help someone move. You will go home early and soak in a hot tub, while others work late. You will have a vacation day at the beach while others remain at home in the rain. Surprisingly and wonderfully, these opportunities often come at times and in ways that you least expect.

Many years ago, at the church in which my husband and I minister, there was a dear and precious man by the name of Wenceslaus Farlow, affectionately known as "Brother Wency." Brother Wency had been a Catholic monk prior to coming to our church. In his desire to serve the Lord fully and humbly in any capacity, he became the church janitor, the Bible college cook and, among other things, was in charge of operating the overhead projector during the worship services on Sunday mornings.

One day the principal of our elementary school asked one of the first graders, "Who do you think is the most important person in our church?" The first grader's response was, "Brother Wency!" When the principal asked the child why he thought the "most important person" was Brother Wency, the child simply said, "Well, he gets to run the overhead projector on Sunday mornings, and he has all the keys!"

Children have such insight! It's true—when we serve faithfully and sacrificially, we will receive "keys to the kingdom." Even this child could see that this servant of all, our dear Brother Wency, was content, happy and had reaped the rewards of great trust from many. Not only did he sacrificially give blessings, but he also reaped blessings. He had all the "keys to the kingdom." What a person of influence he was!

Take Up His Cross

In Luke 9, Jesus goes on to say that you must take up your cross daily. Notice that He does not say that you must take up His cross. He only asks that you take up the cross that relates to your own destiny, purpose and calling.

Jesus used this analogy with His disciples because they understood crucifixion. They understood that crucifixion meant being willing to die the most painful death known to man at that time in history, for the sake of what they believed in.

Jesus Himself knew what crucifixion meant. Historians tell us that when Jesus was eleven years old, Judas the Galilaean led a rebellion against Rome. He and his soldiers raided the royal armory at Sepphoris, which was only four miles from Nazareth, where Jesus lived. As a result, Sepphoris was burned to the ground, its people were sold into slavery and two thousand rebels were crucified. The crosses were set in lines along the roadside as a warning to others against defying Roman authority. I can only imagine that eleven-year-old Jesus walked by those two thousand crosses a number of times and meditated on the message they held. The men of Sepphoris paid a price for what they believed, and it cost them their lives.

Jesus completely understood what He was asking us when He asked it. He was saying that if we are going to take up our cross, we must be willing to endure the worst that man can do for the sake of the cross, the destiny and the calling. He said that we would have to take it up "daily." That means we will have to give love when we have been given harshness, and truth when we have been given lies. We will have to give kindness when we have been given bitterness, and joy when we have been given sorrow. We will need to offer a prayer of healing when we have been given disease and an offering when we have gone without. Yes, there will be an opportunity every day to take up our personal cross for the sake of the call.

Let me say, lest you become faint of heart and determine not to respond to the call, there are rewards. Remember "the keys to the kingdom." They are within your reach.

Follow Me

The third challenge that Jesus brings in this passage is "follow me." Simply put, you cannot follow Him and be totally focused on your own personal agenda at the same time. You really cannot go two directions at once.

The harvest is great. The Master has need of you to work in the harvest. His orders must be followed to work in the field effectively:

deny yourself, take up your cross daily and follow Him. As you fulfill this scripture, people will easily follow your example of conduct. The reason? Your example of conduct will sacrificially have their best interest in mind.

In Love

I Timothy 4:12 adds that we are also to be examples of believers "in love," or by our love. This phrase actually carries with it the picture of a love feast.

People should be able to come to you, as a Christian, and know that they can receive love on a consistent basis. You may not always be able to give people acceptance of their deeds, but you should always be able to give them the love of Christ, simply because they have been created by God. After all, that is what Christ does. We live in such a hate-filled world. As a Christian woman, people should find in you a place of refuge as they follow the Christ in you. That is, indeed, part of your calling.

Of course, there will be times when you won't feel like loving or giving anymore. There will be times when there will be no "feast" left in you. You will feel like the devourers have come and taken all that you have to offer. When the phone rings one more time, you may shout from within, "I already gave at the office!" However, as you continue to follow Christ, He will enable you. He will anoint you to do that which He has called you to do.

Personally, I have found it to be a very beneficial practice to read I Corinthians 13 once a day for a month at least twice a year. The meditation of this passage helps to keep the focus of love flowing through your mind and spirit. His Word is what will faithfully sustain you in times of weariness.

Showing love to people means being genuinely interested in them and having a servant's heart toward them. Many years ago, I read of a college student who was working on his doctorate in sociology. Before writing his doctoral thesis, he was required to live with a Navajo Indian tribe on the reservation for a year. During this time, he spent a significant amount of time with the grandmother of the tribe. She could not speak English and he could not speak her native language. However, each day they spent time together sharing with one another. She taught him weaving and a variety of other skills that were common yet precious to her. He became attached to her and she to him.

On the day that he was to make his final departure from the reservation, he went out to get into the truck without saying goodbye to the grandmother. He simply did not have the heart to bid her farewell, as he knew he would probably never see her again. As he stepped up onto the truck, she came shuffling through the crowd and stood in front of him. She reached up and put her hands on his face, drew him close to her and said, "I like me best when I'm with you."

Somehow, though the student and the grandmother had no common spoken language, they had endeared themselves to one another through the bond of care and kindness–the bond of genuine love. This has been such a meaningful illustration to me through the years. I often ask myself if people somehow feel better about themselves after they have spent time with me–if they have tasted of Christ in some way while they have been with me. Has someone left your presence today feeling personally uplifted because they have been with you–because they have been with the "Christ in you?"

You can never give too much love to people these days. People are love-starved in this generation. There was a little chorus that was sung in our church many years ago that went like this:

You can't out-give the Lord no matter what you do.
You'll find out in the end, the Lord's out-given you.
Your silver and your gold, your love and service too.
You can't out-give the Lord no matter what you do. [1]

I have found this to be true so many times. Yes, there will be people who will hurt you and take advantage of your kindness. But the vast majority of people need the love and kindness of Christ. Most will be grateful for the sharing of it. By your example of generously giving love and kindness, they will learn how to multiply Christ's love and give it freely to one another also. The multiplication principal in the Body of Christ is, indeed, beautiful to behold.

 1. Rob Robbins, Melody Lane Music

In Spirit

"In spirit" means in our mental disposition. The Greek word here is a picture of "a current of air, breath or blast." Proverbs 20:27 says, "The spirit of a man is the lamp of the Lord, searching all the inner depths of his heart." Our spirits are like a light to the Lord, enabling Him to see into the inner depths of our hearts.

In the state of Washington in 1980, Mount St. Helens erupted in a volcanic explosion. Prior to eruption, it was known as the third highest mountain in the northwestern United States. In its second eruption, in one single blast, it went from third place to thirteenth. This is a simple illustration that demonstrates the effect of an uncontrolled or unrestrained spirit. As the "heart" of the mountain blew, it killed people and animals and devastated the land that surrounded it. It also lost some of its prestige in the blowing.

This natural wonder demonstrates a great spiritual lesson. Our spirits must be under the control of the Holy Spirit at all times. Philippians 2:5, 8 says, "Let this mind be in you which was also in Christ Jesus . . . He humbled Himself and became obedient to the point of death . . ." His spirit was under control, as ours can be if we continually yield to Him.

There is a natural ebb and flow to the ocean current. The ebb is its decline; the flow is its push forward. Sometimes, in a moment of emotional decline or of frayed hormones, you can devastate the people "on the beach." When you sense that you have more ebb than flow, it is better to excuse yourself calmly, go to your prayer closet or go rest for awhile than to hurt God's unsuspecting people.

The author of the book of Proverbs charges, ". . . that you incline your ear to wisdom, and apply your heart to understanding . . ." (Proverbs 2:2). This is certainly vital if we are to keep our spirits, our inner persons, under the control of the Holy Spirit.

In Faith

Hebrews 11:6 tells us that "without faith it is impossible to please Him." Hebrews 10:23 says, "Let us hold fast the profession of our faith without wavering, for He is faithful that promised." The "in faith" part of this passage in Timothy stirs us to be women of conviction and constancy; women who are not constantly up and down with uncontrolled emotions and unrestrained mouths, but rather who are constant in faith and full of conviction.

Pastor and author, Charles Simpson, once quoted his father as saying, "Anxiety is a mild case of atheism." I believe that the elder Simpson had a point worth pondering. As women, we know that, all too often, we are given to anxiety and worry. It is crucial that, as Christian women, we have a positive possession of faith. When I say "possession of faith," I choose my words carefully. It is much easier to have a confession of faith than it is to have possession of it. Sadly, if we do not possess it, we will not have free passage to confess it for very long.

People today are looking beyond words and looking for those who truly possess what they profess to believe. They are looking for those who are genuine, joyful and at peace. As contemporary Christians with a desire to be influential, we must develop a deep trust in God. As we find in Philippians, "Be anxious for nothing, but in everything by prayer and supplication, with thanksgiving, let your requests be made know to God; and the peace of God, which surpasses all understanding, will guard your hearts and minds through Christ Jesus" (Philippians 4:6-7).

In Purity

This phrase in Timothy challenges us as women to be chaste in our behavior. Moral purity in behavior is a must for all Christians. Your behavior, as a Christian woman, should never cause anyone to doubt your faithfulness to Christ. If you are married, your behavior should also not cause anyone to doubt your commitment to your husband as well. Privately and consistently meeting late into the evening with a person walking in open sin is unwise for both of you and may harm your Christian example. Also, privately meeting with a member of the opposite sex on any kind of continuing basis is dangerous as well. Both scenarios are seedbeds for temptation, and can cause you to be a very poor example. We will touch on this more in a later chapter.

Is It Worth the Price?

Admittedly, there is a cost involved in being a Christian woman of influence. There are things that you have never been told because your parents, friends or mentors honestly didn't know the Lord's specific agenda for you. The bottom line price is the same for every believer, but the price you will pay will be uniquely marked for your sake, and will also be for the sake of those who are following your example.

When you hear the firm yet gentle "others may, but you may not," rather than chaffing, rejoice and focus on what you can do. Remember Brother Wency and the "keys?" Your sacrificial service and example will not go unnoticed by the Lord.

After all of these challenges in verse twelve of I Timothy four, Paul closes this chapter in verse sixteen with the clear challenge, "Take heed to yourself and to the doctrine. Continue in them, for in doing this you will save both yourself and those who hear you." Think of that reward!

Chapter 3

PRAYER

A Woman of Personal Prayer

W hen I was in my twenties, I realized for the first time that, even as a Christian, one may feel a need to find "a place to hide." It was during a communion service at church. Occasionally, bread was served at communion instead of the standard wafer. This allowed people to break bread together, bless one another and right any wrongs for the sake of unity in the church life.

That evening, the person leading communion read I Corinthians 11:27-34: "Therefore whoever eats this bread or drinks this cup of the Lord in an unworthy manner will be guilty of the body and blood of the Lord. But let a man examine himself, and so let him eat of the bread and drink of the cup. For he who eats and drinks in an unworthy manner eats and drinks judgment to himself, not discerning the Lord's body. For this reason many are weak and sick among you, and many sleep. For if we would judge ourselves, we would not be judged. But when we are judged, we are chastened by the Lord, that we may not be condemned with the world. . . ." The leader then explained that we should not have any offenses among ourselves as we take communion. He allowed those present some time to examine their own hearts and go to anyone with whom they had offenses to clear them up.

With my clear conscience in tact, I was busy praying with people and blessing them. Then a woman came to me to let me know that she had an offense against me. She felt she needed to come to me to get it cleared up. She said I hadn't really done anything wrong, but she had just been offended with me because of my position of leadership in the church. A bit confused, I apologized immediately for causing her offense. I think she genuinely misunderstood the part of the passage that says, "...let a man examine *himself*..." Now she felt great. I felt burdened, awkward, hurt, and I definitely wanted to hide.

The next time we had a "bread-breaking" service in the church, I broke bread with a couple of people sitting nearby and then I slipped away from the sanctuary to use the Ladies' Restroom. No more "bread-baking" services for me–I had been baked enough! Much to my surprise, one of my dear friends, who was also in a place of leadership, was also in the restroom. We began to chat a bit, and I asked her what she was doing in the bathroom. She responded, "Oh, I always come in here during these services. Otherwise, people are lined up just waiting to tell me how they're offended with me!" I couldn't believe my ears! We were both hiding in the bathroom during holy communion!

Well, I no longer hide in the Ladies' Restroom during communion services. I have found a place in Scripture that suits me a little better now. Psalm 17:8 has become one of my favorite verses: "Keep me as the apple of Your eye; hide me under the shadow of Your wings."

Even though I have forgotten who approached me in that long-ago communion service, I do have to admit that my stomach still feels a little queasy every time we have a bread-breaking service. I tell myself that I am supposed to be mature enough to handle this kind of misguided confrontation now. Jesus said, "Father, forgive them, for they do not know what they do" (Luke 22:34). I think this is really true in these kinds of situations also. Sometimes people really do not know how to examine their own hearts. They genuinely have difficulty discerning between self-inflicted offenses and offenses which others have caused. They do not understand when it is appropriate to confront another person and when it is appropriate to just take it to the Lord in prayer.

I think this is a good prayer before a bread-breaking service: "Lord, please help me to be a turtle today." Funny prayer, huh? Whether you find yourself in a capacity of official leadership within the Christian community or not, there will be times when you may need to be like a turtle–hard enough on the outside to deflect arrows sent by Satan, but tender on the inside so that you will remain willing to reach out to people, even the ones who hurt you and judge you wrongfully.

Where Can I Hide When Offenses Come?

Of course, bread-breaking services are not the only times when people may come at you with spears in their hands. You truly need to be a woman of prayer and have a close personal relationship with the Lord in order to serve people with continued tenderness of heart.

Whether those whom you relate to in some leadership capacity are in the workplace, the neighborhood or the church, they will feel the right to speak into your life.

In Luke 17:1, Jesus says, ". . . It is impossible that no offenses should come . . ." Offenses will come. Christianity does not put you in a protective glass bubble. It often provides more opportunities for you to offer healing to wounded people through the avenue of kindness and forgiveness. Actually, serving Christ actively gives you many opportunities to bless people and to be blessed in return. In fact, the blessings far outweigh the difficulties.

However, I would be remiss if I did not mention that even though you may be completely devoted to serving people and making them successful, they will not always love you. The belief that they will is a complete misnomer. People will not always love and appreciate you or your genuine efforts. There may be many times when you will need to find a place of refuge and comfort under the shadow of His wings (Psalm 17:8).

There are times when we all need our own special hiding place. The reality is that there is no place to hide from challenges or misunderstandings. Those will come no matter where you place yourself geographically or emotionally. Some people hide in restrooms, some behind guarded hearts. The safest place to hide is in His presence where refuge and refreshing are found.

The success of your personal life and your ability to minister to others with anointing is dependent upon one of two responses that you make. The first response is in Genesis 3:10, man's first biblically recorded words, "I heard Your voice in the garden, and I was afraid because I was naked; and I hid myself." The second response is Revelation 22:20, man's last biblically recorded words, "Even so, come, Lord Jesus!"

Which will be your response? You have the power of choice; He gives you that in His sovereign will. Often invite Him to walk close to you in your journey. He is the One who called you, and He is the one who prepared the way for you. Wisdom says to stay near to His side.

How Can I Overcome Hindrances to Prayer?

For too long the enemy has kept men and women out of their prayer closets through the avenue of condemnation. I have never met a Christian yet who feels that he or she is "just too close to God."

I am not talking about prayers for the sick or intercessions for the harvest. I am talking about a personal quiet place with God, that place where you repeatedly come to receive personal refreshing and affection from God.

You can be very diligent about praying for your family, your friends, your finances, your church gatherings and the lost souls of your city. You can even be diligent about praying for greater accuracy in your prayers, more anointing on the decisions you make or more effectiveness in the words that you say, all for the sake of the harvest. However, how often do you take time to sit and commune with the Father? How often do you come into a quiet place and listen to what He might want to say? How often do you come to His Word and "selah," simply pause and think about what it says? Sadly, it is probably not as often as you would prefer.

What hinders you from taking that needed time with the Lord? You know, as well as I do the reasons why. You can get so busy meeting the needs of everyone else around you that you do not have time for yourself. You advise others to take the time. You even pray with others that God will multiply their time so that they can meet with Him. However, when it comes to yourself, the enemy whispers in your ears to convince you that you are too self-absorbed, too busy or too tired just to sit in the Father's presence and meditate on His Word.

The enemy will always work hard at trying to convince you that you need to study more, exercise more and work more. "After all," he reasons with you, "the harvest is coming. There is much to be accomplished!" No wonder the Lord said to Jeremiah, "Let not the wise man glory in his wisdom, let not the mighty man glory in his might, nor let the rich man glory in his riches; but let him who glories glory in this that he understands and knows Me, that I am the Lord, exercising lovingkindness, judgment, and righteousness in the earth."

Not only resist the enemy's strategy of works, but also resist the vain counting of minutes and scrutinizing of geographic locations when it comes to your personal time with the Lord. Some of your most intimate moments with the Lord may be in your car while driving down the freeway or late in the evening with your head on your pillow. The enemy wants to convince you that those moments don't count. They do count!

What Can I Learn from Jesus' Example?

Consistent, concentrated times of prayer are also needful in your relationship with the Lord. Jesus was an example of one who consistently had quiet time with the Father. In fact, there came a day, after Jesus had been having His own time of prayer, that one of His disciples came to Him and said, ". . . Lord, teach us to pray . . ." (Luke 11:1).

It was common, at that time, for Rabbis to give their disciples a short prayer to memorize. Two of Jesus' disciples had previously been John the Baptist's disciples, and they had noted to Jesus that John had given them a prayer, so perhaps He should too.

Although this was a common part of the mentoring process of that day, it is interesting to notice that Jesus waited for the disciples to request to be taught. He patiently waited for their hunger. He did not want his disciples, the future leaders of His people, to mindlessly repeat a prayer or mantra. He wanted them to think about what they were praying.

He so yearns for each of us to draw near and have a relationship with Him. He does not want mindless puppets that quote memorized babble. He wants meaningful conversation from the heart. So rather than a simple poetic monologue, He gives His disciples a pattern to follow in their personal prayers.

When You Pray, Talk

In Luke 11:2, Jesus says, "When you pray, say . . ." This is the introduction to the pattern. "When you pray, say . . ." Now, you might not be a Hallelujah-shoutin' person, but the Lord does want you to speak your requests to Him. He does not want you to just think them. Yes, "the Lord knows the thoughts of man . . ." (Psalm 94:11). He knows your thoughts, but He wants to have conversation with you about them.

You don't need to speak your prayers for the Lord to gain knowledge of your concerns. You need to speak them for the sake of relationship with Him. Simply stated, He enjoys conversation. He created each of us in His image; this should give us a clue in this regard. Just as we enjoy conversation with our friends, so God also enjoys conversation with us. As amazing as that may seem, it's true. Hence, whether you are more sanguine or more contemplative by nature, "when you pray, say . . ."

Focus on God and All That He Is

Following this introduction, Jesus tells His disciples to always begin with their focus on God. He tells them to begin, "Our Father in heaven, hallowed be Your name" (Matthew 6:9).

"Father" speaks of your relationship to Him and His relationship to you. By this, Jesus is saying, "Just stop for a moment and focus on this wonderful, caring, nurturing relationship."

"Heaven" speaks of His transcendence. This means, "Now focus on how your very personal Father transcends all." Could anything really be too difficult for Him? See how He gently puts our requests in proper perspective before they are even made?

"Name" speaks of the Father's greatness. Psalm 148:13 says, ". . . His name alone is exalted . . ." Psalm 72:17 says, "His name shall endure forever; His name shall continue as long as the sun. . . ."

Jesus does not just leave the focus on the name, but implies, "Be sure that when you speak to the Father, you say, 'Hallowed be Your name.' " "Hallowed" simply means, "Make sure to approach Him with proper respect."

I was once in a music ensemble that sang a song which included the line, "Hello J.C., how is it going?" "J.C." referred to Jesus Christ. We in no way meant for it to sound disrespectful. However, when one minister heard the words, he corrected our too casual approach to Jesus Christ in this song. Although our attempt was to let it be known that Jesus was approachable, we failed to acknowledge the truth of Philippians 2:9-11: "Therefore God also has highly exalted Him and given Him the name which is above every name, that at the name of Jesus every knee should bow, of those in heaven, and of those on earth, and of those under the earth, and that every tongue should confess that Jesus Christ is Lord, to the glory of God the Father." Jesus is approachable and does want you to speak with personal affection to Him, but He also sets the pattern of respect in prayer.

Notice that He also instructs the disciples to say, "Your name." In other words, "Be respectful, but be endearing." He has given so much. In fact, the Psalmist, in chapter twenty-three and verse one, says, "The Lord is my shepherd; I shall not want." This is a boasting type remark that one sheep is making to another, saying, "I've got the best Master that anyone could ever want. I never have a need that He doesn't meet in some special way. You ought to come join me in my pasture!" The Lord does, indeed, bless and care for His people. Affection and gratitude for our very personal Master should easily pour from our lips.

Posture Yourself to Do His Will and Not Your Own

Next, Jesus tells His disciples, "Always posture yourself to do His will, not your own." He says, in Matthew 6:10, "Be sure to pray, 'Your kingdom come. Your will be done on earth as it is in heaven.' "

Make Temperate Personal Requests

In verse eleven of Matthew six, He gives instruction on how to present daily requests. He encourages the disciples to make a temperate request. He says to pray, "Give us this day our daily bread." In other words, "Give us enough bread for today," or as Luke says, "day by day."

The Israelites in the wilderness learned to eat the manna that the Lord brought to them each day, as the leftover manna always spoiled. Be satisfied with the portion that the Lord brings and be ever mindful to use the surplus He gives to bless others.

Acknowledge Your Need for a Clear Conscience

Jesus goes on to instruct his disciples in humility and the pattern of forgiveness. He says that each disciple should be faithful to acknowledge his need for a clear conscience. In verse twelve of Matthew six, He continues, "And forgive us our debts, as we forgive our debtors." Romans 7:18-19 says, "For I know that in me (that is, in my flesh) nothing good dwells; for to will is present with me, but how to perform what is good I do not find. For the good that I will to do, I do not do; but the evil I will not to do, that I practice."

Humility is needed. There is no good in any of us apart from Christ. As you acknowledge this in humility, then grace is applied to your heart and you will be able to forgive others for their faults as well. Ephesians 4:32 says, "Be kind to one another, tenderhearted, forgiving one another, even as God in Christ forgave you." This is one of those verses that is worth memorizing and engraving on the tablet of your heart.

Acknowledge Your Reaction to Evil

Next, Jesus emphasizes the need to acknowledge a reaction to evil. In verse thirteen of this passage, he teaches, "And do not lead us into temptation, but deliver us from the evil one." You must express your desire to be delivered from the influence of the evil one, Satan himself. Be discerning of the varying influences that surround you; honestly admit their effect and be willing to take a stand against those influences or remove yourself from their target base. Whether it is unedifying entertainment, gossip or sensual behavior, your response must be the same. "Deliver me from the evil one" must be your cry.

Focus on God and Renew Your Commitment To His Purposes

The closing portion of Christ's prayer pattern is to be sure to focus on God again. In verse thirteen of Matthew six, Jesus says, "Close with this: 'For Yours is the kingdom and the power and the glory forever. Amen.'" "Kingdom" represents purpose. "Power" represents our source and strength. "Glory" represents motive. Jesus says to close by proclaiming,

"God, You are my purpose in life! You are my source and strength! You are my motive, my reason for continuing on!"

Then He says, "Oh yes, and close it off with a big 'Amen.' " This is simply a renewed commitment to do something about what you have just talked about. By this, you are saying, "I'm going to give myself to this. I want these things to be true for me today. I commit myself to the tangible fulfillment of these requests. So be it."

How Can I Find Refreshing in the Lord's Presence?

Even though Jesus teaches the disciples this pattern of prayer, He also demonstrated by His life that every moment with God counts. Relationship with Him is made up of anointed moments, divine encounters and deliberately planned sessions. One is not more significant to God than the other. He simply wants you to spend meaningful time with Him so that you might hear His voice clearly and tenderly. The hearing of His voice guides, strengthens and refreshes.

It is very interesting to note that the last miracle Jesus did while He walked on this earth was to heal a soldier's ear. Some would say that this was His most insignificant miracle. Think about it for a moment. He was on His way to the cross, and He was concerned about someone's ability to hear. Oh, how He loves each of us and desires that we are able to clearly hear His voice!

You cannot effectively walk in the anointing of God and serve people for very long if your hearing is deafened and your spiritual tank is empty. There will be times when you are absolutely desperate for time away with the Lord. Your nerves will be frazzled and your spirit weak. Then a knock at the door will come or the phone will ring with a person in need of a touch from the Master. In that moment, God will amazingly pour His anointing upon you, and you will minister with incredible grace. Never misunderstand what this is—it is in these moments that you are truly experiencing His amazing grace! Never take it for granted.

Yes, God loves us enough to anoint us, even when we have not found time in our schedules to be renewed in His presence. However, He also loves us enough not to let us run on empty for too long.

You can face any challenge if you have discovered this precious, personal, quiet place in your relationship with the Master. He never promised any of His servants in the Bible an easy journey, but He did promise that He would be with them.

In Genesis 28:15, we read God's promise to Jacob, "Behold, I am with you and will keep you wherever you go . . ." Jacob received this promise, with a rock for his pillow, as he dreamed of the angels of God ascending and descending between heaven and earth on a ladder. When he awoke early the next morning, he ". . . took the stone that he had put at his head, set it up as a pillar, and poured oil on top of it. And he called the name of that place Bethel [House of God]" (Gen. 28:18-19).

Is not Jesus the "rock of my salvation" (Psalm 89:26)? Is He not the One who has given us "access by faith into this grace in which we stand" (Romans 5:1-2)? Is He not the Anointed One of God? Truly, Jesus is your Rock, your Ladder and your means to the Father. It is in His very presence that the anointing oil will flow and then be poured out through you in His House.

Jesus will continually beckon you to come away with Him and allow Him to fill you afresh with His presence. In His kindness and graciousness toward you He wants to affirm you and fill you with renewed confidence in order that you can continue the journey that He has called you to. It is under the shadow of His wings and in His presence that His refreshing comes. His presence is like a fresh, spring rain that will pour over your soul. Draw near often and "walk in newness of life" (Romans 6:4). Your anointing comes from abiding in His presence.

Chapter 4

FAITH
A Woman Who Triumphs over Disappointment

Disappointment sets foot on the doorstep of every believer at some time in life. It cloaks itself in a variety of ways. Sometimes it is the work of the enemy of our souls, sometimes the result of a personal insufficiency and sometimes the faithful working of our very personal God. However when disappointment comes, it usually releases within us a deeper revelation of our need to draw near to our Master and Lord.

Why Does the Lord Allow Disappointment in My Life?

No one is exempt from facing contradictions in his or her life. In fact, sometimes you will be more of a target for disappointment if you are in a place of influence. The enemy attacks because he wants to discourage and destroy you. You can even create your own dilemmas, at times, simply because you are not perfect. The Lord may compassionately allow these times because He wants to mature you. He does this for your personal learning and for the sake of those you are called to influence.

As a Christian, there is almost always someone watching at times like these. It seems to be a part of our calling. The onlooker may be a nurse in the hospital or a neighbor next door, but usually someone is watching to see if something you face can relate to a similar circumstance of life that he or she is experiencing.

No matter how old you are in Christ or how many years you spend serving Him, you will find that He will continue to work in your heart. He will do this with great grace through your circumstances to give you a very precious gift–an educated heart. There is no better educator than Jesus the Master Teacher.

He will also allow certain disappointments to come your way for the sake of greater fruitfulness in your life. If you will allow His breaking to work in you He will use this and your educated heart to be the food of compassion and understanding for others.

One of the most hope-filled passages of the Old Testament, in times of personal disappointment, is Isaiah 45:2-3. It says, "I will go before you and make the crooked places straight; I will break in pieces the gates of bronze and cut the bars of iron. I will give you the treasures of darkness and hidden riches of secret places, that you may know that I, the Lord who calls you by your name, am the God of Israel."

I am not going to attempt to interpret this verse. However, I would like to apply it to our daily lives. Regardless of the disappointments that you may face, if you will hold tightly to the Lord, He will not only deliver you and heal you from the hurt of the circumstance, but He will also reveal Himself to you. He will give you treasures and hidden riches from His secret place, in the midst of the dark places of confusion. These treasures will enrich your soul personally and will be food for others who are hurting.

Disappointment may come to you in a variety of ways. Perhaps you can relate to some of these examples provided in the following list.

DISAPPOINTMENTS

- You have planned a busy day, and the car won't run.
- You have saved just enough money to buy that new dress, and your child suddenly needs to go to the doctor and the money goes with him.
- You are dressed and manicured for a much-needed romantic evening with your husband, and unexpected guests greet you at the door.
- Your teenager has been arrested for drug abuse.
- Your husband has admitted to being unfaithful.
- You have purchased the much-desired pregnancy test at the store, only to arrive home just in time for your monthly cycle to start.
- You have purchased that new spring dress, but much to your dismay, it's one size larger than last year's.
- You have reached twenty-nine, and "Mr. Right" has not yet set foot on your doorstep.
- You have reached thirty, and your hormones have shown up in full bloom. You explode at your faithful friend and coddle the new grouchy neighbor down the street.
- You go to the podium on Sunday morning to announce the next women's meeting, and when you get there, you can't remember what you are supposed to announce.
- You have finally gotten the weight off, purchased the new dress that you've been saving six months for, and when you get to church, you see three other women with the same dress on. You smile at each of them and then promptly spill communion juice down the front of your dress.
- You have recently lost your own child, when both a young, single teenager and a mother of five announce the arrival of their newborns.
- You have made soup for the tenth Sunday in a row to save on the cost of groceries, and a wealthy businessman's wife asks you to pray for her husband's prosperity for the sake of their children's inheritance.
- You have just learned that your teen has been diagnosed with a terminal illness.
- You have taught your best Sunday school lesson, and a child comes to you proudly after the class with a tally score of how many times you said "uh" when you were speaking.
- You have come to the realization that your daily schedule never really does end, and no one is offering you a big salary for it.

The list could go on and on. Three things are certain: the enemy is always at work, the Lord is always at work and the revelation of our own ignorance shows up when we least expect it. Perhaps three more things are also certain: you need the freedom to pray, laugh and cry when needed as you walk this journey to its end.

How Can I Change My Perspective in the Face of Disappointment?

The bottom line here is that disappointment often comes when expectations and reality meet head on. Unyielded expectations will always collide with the working of the Holy Spirit in our lives. Romans 8:28-32 says, "And we know that all things work together for good to those who love God, to those who are the called according to His purpose. For whom He foreknew, He also predestined to be conformed to the image of His Son, that He might be the firstborn among many brethren. Moreover whom He predestined, these He also called; whom He called, these He also justified; and whom He justified, these He also glorified. What then shall we say to these things? If God is for us, who can be against us? He who did not spare His own Son, but delivered Him up for us all, how shall He not with Him also freely give us all things?"

You must continually be willing to yield your perspective of your anticipated life course and embrace what comes in your direction. God's definition of "good" may often differ from your definition. My husband interprets the "good," in this passage, as "change and growth," rather than "comfort and ease." In other words, your definition of "good" may be that "all things should work together to make your life comfortable and easy." God's definition, however, is meant to work for your "change and growth." God's aim is to process you and transform you into the image of His Son, as it says here in Romans chapter eight. He is not overly concerned about your continued comfort, but He is concerned about your continued change and growth in Him. This is crucial for walking in His calling and anointing. He is very interested in transforming you into His image. If you will yield to this process you will become more like Him, and that definitely will be "good."

Jeremiah 29:11 says, "For I know the plans that I have for you, declares the Lord, plans for welfare and not for calamity, to give you a future and a hope" (NAS). This is another tremendous, hope-filled promise. Think of it! God actually has a plan that is going to project you into a future that is filled with hope!

How Am I to Handle Disappointment?

Of course, prior to embracing this bright future, you must embrace the present and release the past. You must appropriately handle the disappointments that will come your way. How you do this will affect you personally and will affect those to whom you minister, whether they are family members, friends or others.

Know Who You Are

First of all, know who you are. Herein lies the great battle for women today. The world around you will demand that you know who you are as a person and as a woman.

People everywhere are crying out to know who they are and where they are going. If we, as Christian men and women, don't know ourselves, then the world is lost. That sounds frightening, doesn't it?!

Allow me to ask these questions. What part of your identity, as a person or a woman, can never be taken from you? What part of your identity is not based on how you function or to whom you are related? Hidden within the answer to these two questions is the revelation of who you are as a person. Without this understanding, you will crumble in the face of severe disappointment. You will sadly discover that you can become emotionally paralyzed and unable to function appropriately as one of God's servants.

John 13:3-4 tells us, "Jesus, knowing that the Father had given all things into His hands, and that he had come from God and was going to God, rose from supper and laid aside His garments, took a towel and girded Himself." The following verses speak of Jesus serving the disciples by washing their feet. He knew the greatest trial of His life was coming and that some of them would betray Him. What a disappointment this must have been after the faithfulness that He had poured out to them! Yet because He knew where He had come from and where He was going, He could serve them. He remembered who He was in the midst of the contradiction. He knew what portion of His identity could not be taken from Him by any person or under any circumstance.

Throughout your lifetime, the way, the place and the people to whom you minister may change. Even your friendships and family relationships may change to varying degrees. Some will change with the seasons of life. Some will change for reasons that you understand and some for reasons that you will never understand. One way or the other, change will come. Change is the constant you can count on.

Sometimes change will come in the form of no change. There may be times when you are anxiously expecting change. You are praying and hoping for it, but it refuses to come. When that happens, look for the change to occur from within.

Following an overseas trip, my husband became ill for over seven years. Whatever he had contracted was as mysterious to the doctors as it was to us. During that time, I prayed for change, hoped for change, demanded change and cried for change. However, the outward change that I was looking for was slow in coming. Over the course of seven years, many changes occurred in both my husband and myself. They were not the changes that were obvious to the casual observer, but they were changes from deep within.

Change is the reliable constant in life. It may come to you in a different form than you are expecting, but it will come. You must be careful in the midst of change never to confuse your identity with your role or function. Roles and functions may change, but your identity in Christ never will.

Corrie Ten Boom, who has now gone to be with the Lord, is an esteemed woman of God in contemporary church history. As a single adult woman, she, her father and her elder sister helped Jewish people escape from the German persecution during World War II by hiding them in their home in Holland. Corrie was also a clock-maker in her father's clock shop. One day, the German soldiers invaded Corrie's home and took her, her sister and her father to a prison camp. Her father died, and soon after she and her sister entered the prison, her sister also died. During this time, Corrie was neither a rescuer of the Jewish people nor a clock-maker. In an earthly sense, she was no longer a daughter or a sister. What part of Corrie Ten Boom's identity could not be taken from her while she was in prison camp? Her identity in Christ, of course, was the only part that they could not affect or steal from her. She remained a daughter of the King of Kings, regardless of her earthly circumstance. So it is with you. Today you may be the primary worship leader of your church; tomorrow your voice could begin to crack and go off key when you least expect it. Today you may be a single executive; tomorrow you may be married to a man who wants a stay-at-home wife. Today you could be a supervisor with a full-time salary; tomorrow the budget could crash and you will be free to volunteer your services. Today you could be a mother with children all around you; tomorrow your children may decide to serve God on the other side of the ocean. Today you could be an office executive; tomorrow a younger, more motivational person may replace you. Today you may be thirty years old; tomorrow you will discover that you are sixty-five, and people expect you to retire. Again, the list could go on and on.

The point is that in whatever part of the journey you are, no disappointment or season in life can take from you this defining part of your identity. You may not be a minister listed in the church directory, an esteemed teacher, counselor, wife or mother. You may not be "young and with it" or "old and wise," but you are, and always will be (if you choose to be), a daughter of the King of Kings.

It is this knowledge of who you are in Christ that is the cornerstone of appropriately handling the disappointments that will certainly come your way.

Be Honest with Yourself

Secondly, when disappointment comes your way, be honest with yourself about it. You will not be able to admit the reality of the disappointment to the Lord or to anyone else if you cannot even be honest with yourself. Job said to his wife, in Job 2:10, ". . . 'Shall we indeed accept good from God, and shall we not receive adversity?' In all this Job did not sin with his lips." If you read this book of the Bible thoroughly, you will discover that Job was in the midst of the ultimate bad day when he said this. At this point, I think he said this to himself as much as to his wife. He needed to acknowledge the facts of the situation to himself. In doing so, he would then be able to acknowledge his disappointment to God, the One who could handle it.

Admit Your Perspective To The Lord

Thirdly, admit your perspective to the Lord. Job 7:11 says, "Therefore I will not restrain my mouth; I will speak in the anguish of my spirit; I will complain in the bitterness of my soul." Job was really being transparent here. At times like this, in your life and ministry, you will also need to be transparent with the Lord. Transparency is another seeming requirement of the call. If you are not transparent with Him, you may hear yourself complaining against the Lord to others. That kind of complaining not only lacks benefit, but is also sin. Only by keeping the communication lines open between you and God will you be able to check a complaining attitude before it begins.

In admitting your perspective to the Lord, be willing to accept God's response or lack of response. After Job exploded to the Lord, God very simply came along and gave Job a zoology lesson. It seemed as though He was ignoring Job's pain. It seemed as though He didn't hear Job's question "why?" behind the complaint. God always hears–be sure of that. He just doesn't always feel obligated to respond in the manner in which we might expect Him to. He simply doesn't find it necessary to be our servant and explain every detail of what goes on in heaven. It seems as though He is bent on engraving in our minds the fact that He is the "creator" and we are the "created." Very simply, it is as though He wants us to trust Him in whatever comes our way.

In Genesis 32:22-32, Jacob found himself in a wrestling match with a Messenger from the Lord. The Messenger marked him by knocking his hip socket out of joint, and then He told Jacob to release Him. Jacob said, "I will not let You go unless You bless me!" This sounds smart, doesn't it? How often do you ask God for a blessing in the midst of a storm? How often have you said to God, "Well, if you're not going to tell me why this is happening, at least bless me in it." When you ask for a blessing in the midst of a trial be ready to answer God's question.

Before the Messenger pronounced a blessing on Jacob, He presented Jacob with a question: "What is your name?" In other words, "Admit to me your perspective on your life." So Jacob responded by giving his name. He was acknowledging the fact that he had been named "supplanter" or "cheater" and that he had, indeed, lived up to his name. The Messenger then gave the divine exchange and said, "Your name shall no longer be called Jacob, but Israel; for you have struggled with God and with men, and have prevailed." Israel means "prince." Through one simple honest admission to God, Jacob's name, and his perspective on his life, was changed from "cheater" to "prince."

Blessing in the midst of seemingly unanswered prayer is God's amazing grace. When you are wrestling with your perspective on yourself and your circumstances, admit it to God, and get the divine exchange that He has in mind for you. You may not always get an explanation, but you can always receive a divine touch if you will reach up in transparency.

You may often advise others in their time of need, "Just be honest with God about it!" You should not say this unless you are an example of it yourself. Being continually honest with God keeps your spirit clean. Simply said, confession is good for the soul.

Release the Disappointment to God

The next crucial step is to give the disappointment to God. Disappointments may come into your life that only God can handle. If you don't give these to Him, they will become unbearable weights that will pull you down into the pit of despair. Sadly, when you are in a place of influence, others may also follow you in deciding to give up their only hope.

My wonderful mother-in-law is an incredible example of one who has completely given herself and her every disappointment to God. She was a beautiful, young singer and pianist in Bible college when my father-in-law met her. They married, spent a year as youth pastors at a church, had their first son and then went to pastor a church in another city. Everything about the future looked bright. No sacrifice for the Lord was too small for them. She was the church pianist, and her husband was the pastor. They were now expecting their second child. The blessings of God were sweet to their souls.

Then one day, during the third month of her pregnancy, she found that she was unable to get out of bed. She had contracted polio. Due to her physical incapacity, the church decided to end their term of service. By the time her pregnancy came to the seventh month, their beautiful baby girl was born without life.

This incredible servant of the Lord, in the beauty of her youth and faithful service to the Lord, became paralyzed in her natural walk, lost her baby and lost her ministry function.

In the early season of this tremendous disappointment, she wrote an anointed chorus that went across the nation in their fellowship of churches:

There's no defeat in Jesus.
He's purchased the victory for me.
Whatever the test or the trial,
There's victory in Jesus for me. [1]

Choice came knocking at her door. She could choose to become bitter and never serve God or His people again, or she could choose to give her disappointment to God and let Him do His work in her. She is still serving the Lord today with her husband of nearly fifty years. Together they are pastors and leaders of the senior citizens in a church. She is a sweet fragrance, not only to the Lord, but also to her family, including the two children born to her following this experience. She also blesses many in prayer, encouragement and counsel. She did not really lose her ministry–it was just redefined and expanded over the years in ways that she might never have imagined at the time.

Remember, our functions do not define our callings. God's will does.

As trials, contradictions, disappointments and unanswerable questions come to you, choice will faithfully come knocking soon after. Plan on it. Be prepared for it. Choose to give your problems to the Master, and absorb the revelation that there is no defeat in Jesus. Accept the fact that you cannot control the circumstances of your life, but you can control your responses to the circumstances.

God is ordering your steps. Gently shift yourself into neutral gear, like you would a car, and let Him drive you around. Give Him control. He is the only one who really knows the detailed pathway of your journey. When your heart is overwhelmed and your mind is a-whirl, "Commit your works to the Lord, and your thoughts will be established" (Proverbs 16:3).

Trust God to Work It Out

Lastly, whatever the circumstance may be, trust God to work it out for His glory. He is the One who called you to this position, and He is the One to trust with the outworking of it. Psalm 37:5 says, "Commit your way to the Lord, trust also in Him, and He shall bring it to pass." Philippians 1:6 says, "Being confident of this very thing, that He who has begun a good work in you will complete it until the day of Jesus Christ." Daniel 6:23 says, ". . . So Daniel was taken up out of the den, and no injury whatever was found on Him, because he believed in His God." It was after the painful insurrection of David's son, Absalom, David wrote in Psalm 23:1, "The Lord is my shepherd; I shall not want." His trust was in the Lord, not in his circumstance.

All of these powerful verses challenge us to trust the Lord to work His will in us and through us, regardless of what the circumstances look like.

Leah is such an incredible example of a woman who trusted in her God when there was no one else to trust. Her father, Laban, deceived Jacob into marrying her due to Jacob's lack of understanding of the marital customs in their culture. Jacob was surprised by Laban's deception and did not have much regard for Leah. In fact, Genesis 29:18 clearly says, "Now Jacob loved Rachel . . ." There was no doubt about the situation. Rachel was the loved wife, and Leah was the wife of obligation.

But Leah had a call. This was a call that neither her father nor her husband understood. Her name is defined as "tender eyed" or "married." Leah was married to Jacob, not only out of obligation, but also out of trust in the Lord. Her children are a clear illustration of her calling.

She named her firstborn son "Reuben," and declared in Genesis 29:32, ". . . The Lord has surely looked on my affliction. Now therefore, my husband will love me." "Reuben" is literally defined "behold a son." In Old Testament history, a son was the very best gift that a wife could give to her husband. Leah was saying, "Look Jacob, a son! Won't you love me now?!"

Leah's second son was named "Simeon," which means "hearing." This Hebrew word is translated "obedient" in the Greek, and is the same word used to describe Jesus in Philippians 2:8: ". . . He humbled Himself and became obedient to the point of death, even the death of the cross."

Christ was listening to the voice of the Father on His walk to the cross, and Leah was obedient to the voice of the Father in her marriage relationship. Obedience and listening go together like a hand in a glove. I believe that Leah was listening very closely to the voice of God as she walked through this seeming contradiction in her marriage. Through her hearing came the grace to be obedient to the call.

Leah's third son was Levi. "Levi" is defined "joined." Perhaps Jacob had become more attentive and joined to her in spirit. It is hard to know, as there is no clear indication of this in Scripture. Perhaps, this was Leah's faith stance.

Her fourth son was Judah. "Judah" means "praise." Judah was her prize, her reward for faithfulness. Judah was the seed to the line of Jesus Christ, the fulfillment of her calling. It was through her, the wife whose life was full of contradiction and disappointment that the seed of promise came for the lost world.

Leah did have two more sons and a daughter following these four. We never have any clear indication that Jacob was ever married to Leah in any loving sense. Scripture only says that he loved Rachel. It does seem clear, though, that Leah truly loved and was married–spirit, soul and body–to Jacob. As challenging and difficult as it was, she accepted her call and trusted God in it.

What Is the Response of Faith?

As a member of the Body of Christ, you do not have the privilege of carrying a past hurt or a present offense into the future with you. There will always be people, on the other side of your offense or trial, waiting and watching for the sake of your example. They may even follow in your footsteps through their own trials or disappointments and quote your name as their example. What will they do, and how will they quote you? These are questions worth pondering.

Jesus paid the price for the hurts so that you could go on in renewed hope and be His instrument in leading others.

He ended His life here on earth saying, "Father, into Your hands I commit My spirit." Let this also be your continual confession of trust. It is this confession that will not only sustain you through the contradictions in your journey, but will also project you to a necessary faith level in the midst of the disappointments.

Chapter 5

OVERCOMING
A Woman Who Gets Back Up

In the previous chapter, we talked about how to handle disappointments brought by others or allowed by God. Now let's talk about the times when you will disappoint yourself. It is in these times that your soul must cry out, "Do not rejoice over me, my enemy; when I fall, I will arise; when I sit in darkness, the Lord will be a light to me. I will bear the indignation of the Lord, because I have sinned against Him, until He pleads my case and executes justice for me. He will bring me forth to the light; I will see His righteousness" (Micah 7:8-9).

These times will be painful. To others your failures may seem insignificant, but to you they will loom large on the horizon. They will be your most embarrassing moments. You will not mention them to others, even when sharing on a personal level. You will tell yourself many times that you should have been stronger than to have yielded to temptation. The memories will bring condemnation, guilt and shame to your spirit. You will try to erase them from your mind, but they will resurface when you least expect them to. You may even fear that, if known to others, these failures would disqualify you from the call.

This all sounds so depressing, so foreboding, but even the strongest of Christian women will experience some kind of personal failure. There will be times when you will stray from your Christian goals and personal ideals. I am not necessarily talking about wounding experiences caused by others, that might thrust you into deep depression or motivate you to backslide. I am referring to your own failures with personal sin. Whether the failure is small or large, it will seem large to you because it is yours.

How Can I Recognize Temptation?

Temptation can come through a variety of avenues: naïve perspective, willful intention, reaction to hurt or satanic attack. Whatever the reason, it is crucial to be spirit-led, not emotion-led. Your emotions are meant to serve you and to be a blessing. However, if you allow your emotions to lead you, they may deceive you. Emotions do not always react with accuracy to outward circumstances.

When temptation to stray from the will of God comes, you will initially have an inner response to that temptation. At that point, you will have to make a choice in regard to that initial inner response, and this will determine your behavioral reaction. You will have an opportunity to consider the work of the cross and all that it means. The next step will be understanding the reality of your choice and responding to your decision. Usually, you will have another opportunity to make a choice, and this will secure your initial decision. From that point on, you will experience the results of your choices.

Personal failure never happens in an instant. It is a process of conscious, emotionally based or willfully based decisions. Consider this chart.

RESPONSES TO TEMPTATION

"Emotion-led Woman"	Temptation Due to: Naïve Perspective Willful Intention Reaction to Hurt Satanic Attack	"Spirit-led Woman"
Internalize & Justify Proverbs 18:19; 15:13; 17:22	Initial Inner Response	Respond to God's Word & the Holy Spirit Psalm 73:28 Respond to Personal Moral Code Jeremiah 17:9; Proverbs 4:7; Romans 8:14; Hebrews 11:25
Forsake Discernment & Succumb to Temptation Proverbs 2:17; 14:1	Point of Choice	Run, Resist & Rebuke I Corinthians 5:11-13; 6:18
Forsake Personal Moral Code Romans 6:20, 21	Behavioral Reaction	Stand on Conviction of the Will Ephesians 2:10; II Corinthians 10:5
Reject Christ & His Principles—FALL Romans 6:23; Revelation 28:14	Identification with the Cross of Christ	Repent & Receive Forgiveness Romans 7:18-19; Jeremiah 31:34; Psalm 57:17
Harden Heart Proverbs 21:29; 29:1	Understanding of Choices	Re-sensitize Conscience Psalm 51:10-12; 95:8; Colossians 3:1-5
Sear Conscience & Continue Spiral Downward I Timothy 4:1-2; Titus 1:15	Point of Choice	Renew & Regenerate the Mind Romans 12:2; 8:1-2; James 1:22; Psalm 119
Become Apostate & Reprobate—BROKEN Romans 1:28; II Timothy 3:5, 8; Titus 1:16	Result Fruit of Choices Made	Find Wholeness, Healthy Self-discovery, Freedom to Serve Others with Love & Confidence I Corinthians 6:11; I Peter 1:22; Philippians 1:6

65

You can see from this chart that God will continually give you opportunities to make a choice and reverse the spiral downward when temptation comes. He leaves each choice up to you. That is His moral will. It is a gift, but one that should be handled with care and with prayer.

How Can I Resist Temptation?

As one called to be an example of the believer, you must be very careful that you don't make yourself easily vulnerable to deeds of sin. As I stated at the beginning of this chapter, there may be times of personal failure that will come into your life. However, you must do your best to live your life in such a way as to have as few regrets as possible.

Be Accountable to Someone

Purpose to keep yourself in accountable relationships with wise friends. Everyone needs friends. Any one of us can fall. I Corinthians 10:12 says, "Therefore let him who thinks he stands take heed lest he fall." Proverbs 11:2 says, "When pride comes, then comes shame; but with the humble is wisdom." Godly friends will help to keep you on the straight and narrow when you may be tempted to stray.

Avoid Loneliness

Don't allow yourself to wallow in loneliness and yield to carnal desires. Keep yourself attached to the Word of God and to His personal presence; this is primary to the call. Also keep yourself busy when you are in a season of loneliness.

When my husband travels, I always have a plan for accomplishing some extra goals while he's gone. Whether it's wallpapering a room, doing some special studies or spending extra time with my children or friends, I stay busy.

There is a difference between being alone and being lonely. Single adult women, who live on their own, are alone, but they are not necessarily lonely. Loneliness is often a key in the formula for a moral fall, not aloneness. However, constantly being alone has the potential for failure also. This is true for married women and single women alike.

Being alone too often leaves you to your own thoughts and perspectives without a balancing perspective. The wisest, single adult women I know are women who are not only busy about Kingdom business, but who also have friends. Their friends are people with whom they have fun and with whom they also have meaningful, accountable relationships.

Do Not Yield to Carnal Influence

When you come across a person who is not focused on the will of God, no matter what position this individual may hold, do not yield yourself to his or her influence. Even if this person attempts to seduce you, cover yourself with the Lord's Word and flee. I Corinthians 6:18 says, "Flee sexual immorality." Your primary responsibility is to the Lord and His Word, not to another person.

What Should I Do if I Fail?

Repent Immediately

If you do fall, repent immediately. I John 1:9 says, "If we confess our sins, He is faithful and just to forgive us our sins and to cleanse us from all unrighteousness." Then, confess to the persons you sinned against or to a Christian leader you can trust. James 5:16 tells us, "Confess your trespasses to one another, and pray for one another, that you may be healed. The effective, fervent prayer of a righteous man avails much."

Respond in Humility

Notice, in John 21:15-19, that Jesus tells Peter to feed His sheep after he fails, not before. It was after the failure that compassion entered Peter's soul. Failure had made Peter tender. It had given him revelation of God's abundant grace and unconditional love through the avenue of forgiveness. It had made him humbly aware of his own frailty. Once again, we see that humility is a key to a successful walk.

Jeremiah 31:3-4 says, ". . . I have loved you with an everlasting love;

I have drawn you with loving kindness. I will build you up again and you will be rebuilt . . ." (NIV). Failure will pull you down if you don't make it work for good in you. It is God's love that will restore you and do the work in and through you.

Resist the Accuser

During these times of personal failure, the enemy of your soul, Satan himself, will attack. He will berate you and attempt to completely defeat you. Satan's greatest joy is not to just knock you down, but to knock you out of the playing field.

History tells us that, in the early 1500s, the Mayan Indians once inhabited the ancient city of Antigua, Guatemala. They were known as very fierce warriors. Their weapons were bows and arrows, which they used skillfully. One day, the Spaniards came to make war against them. They had weapons, such as swords and guns that the Mayan Indians had never seen or battled against before. The Spaniards also had horses, which the Mayans had never seen before. During battle, the Mayans shot at the horses, thinking that the man and the horse were one and the same. When the horse fell, the rider would quickly jump off and overcome his enemy. The Mayans were defeated because they failed to recognize who the real enemy was. The real enemy was not the horse, but the rider.

When failure comes into your life, you must be careful to recognize who the real enemy is. The enemy is not the failure. The enemy is the author of the failure. It is the one who comes at you after the fall to defeat you completely. Resist the accusations of Satan or anyone else he uses to bring up your past to you.

What if I Feel Like Quitting?

Failure will not revoke your anointing or effectiveness for Christ; quitting will. The worst failure is not getting back up. Do not yield yourself to the impulse to quit. Quitting is not part of the call and definitely lacks the anointing of the Lord.

However, "not quitting" doesn't mean that you should try to pick yourself back up in your own strength. That would be a temporary solution. During these dark and confusing times, you will gain a deep awareness of who you really are, and you will come to know that it is only by His absolute, unconditional love that you can stand. It is by God's grace that you are saved, and it is by His grace and unfailing love, that you must not only stand, but also walk on.

One of the biggest errors in dealing with personal failure is focusing on the one who failed rather than on the One who forgives and restores. You cannot talk about failure without talking about God's tremendous, unfailing love. Only by grasping hold of God's everlasting love can you get back up on your spiritual feet again. It's His love that lifts you back up, not your own strength.

Who in Scripture Illustrates This Cycle of Failure and Repentance?

When you think of women in the Bible who are known for their failure more than their success, Bathsheba is probably the woman who comes to mind first. It's a shame that moral failure is the primary focus of our memory of Bathsheba because this season of failure was really only one year of her life. There actually is so much more to her story. She was a daughter of covenant who got back up.

I Corinthians 10:11-12 tells us, "Now all these things happened to them as examples, and they were written for our admonition, upon whom the ends of the ages have come. Therefore let him who thinks he stands take heed lest he fall." Come, let us learn from Bathsheba.

Bathsheba was born into a God-fearing, financially secure family. Her father Eliam, whose name means "God is gracious," was one of David's gallant officers. Her grandfather Ahithophel was one of King David's faithful counselors. He later became one of Absalom's counselors; then, upon seeing that Absalom's plot was doomed to fail, he hung himself. However, this all happened after Bathsheba's personal failure. Overall, Bathsheba came from a lineage faithful to God and to King David.

Her very name means "the daughter of an oath," denoting the effect of covenant understanding in her family. Her name also means "the seventh daughter," and "daughter of wealth or abundance." She, obviously, was a blessed and cherished daughter.

She was married to Uriah, whose name means "Jehovah is light." He is also listed as one of David's thirty honored guards, his mighty men, his chief men.

Her father, grandfather, and husband all served King David together. They guarded and protected David and fought for his purposes. She had grown up in a family and married into a family that was dedicated to serving King David and obeying his orders.

Now, let's look at a formula for failure as it was walked out in Bathsheba's life.

She Was Naïve, Immodest and Perhaps Lonely

II Samuel 11:2 says, "Then it happened one evening that David arose from his bed and walked on the roof of the king's house. And from the roof he saw a woman bathing, and the woman was very beautiful to behold."

Bathsheba was probably very young and naive at the time of her failure. The average marriageable age for a girl at this time was twelve to sixteen. She may have also been lonely since her husband was away in battle, and they had no children. The Scriptural text tells us that she was very beautiful.

The king, who should have been at the battle, was home, being negligent of his kingly duties. Springtime was the time when kings went to war. Bathsheba was bathing in her own courtyard, which would have been secluded from all ordinary observation, yet visible from the palace roof.

Some researchers would like to make her innocent at this point. However, I am not easily convinced of her innocence. She knew that her courtyard was within view of the palace and that David was home from battle. I am not suggesting that she purposely bathed at a time when she knew David would be looking. However, I'm not sure that she was totally unaware of his habits either. I imagine the neighborhood gossip was as voluminous then as it is today.

She Was Easily Influenced and Yielded Without Protest

II Samuel 11:4 says, ". . . she came to him, and he lay with her . . ." As a woman, she was, by the cultural standards, the lowliest subject of a king. She genuinely had no choice but to obey. However, David was known as being a reasonable man. It could easily be assumed that she knew how Abigail had appealed to David's reason and how he heeded her caution (see I Samuel 25). (Women know things like that!) I am guessing, but I think that if she had really wanted to make an appeal, she would have. If she had, it might have been a different story.

She Concealed the Sin from Her Husband

In II Samuel chapter twelve, Nathan, the prophet, came to reveal the sin of David and Bathsheba to David. Not only had David tried to hide the sin, but Bathsheba had also. Even when her husband had come to the city at David's order, she did not request to see him to make confession. Uriah was the faithful husband with whom she had broken covenant, yet we see no evidence of confession at this point.

She Was Co-Responsible with David in Sin

II Samuel 12:9-14 records God's judgment through Nathan, the prophet, to David and Bathsheba. David held the greater responsibility. However, Bathsheba received the judgment for her own sin as well. She was co-responsible for the judgment that came not only to her own house, but also to the house of David.

Bathsheba paid a price for her disobedience to God's will. Uriah was murdered; her firstborn son by David died; and never again was there peace in David's kingdom after their sin. Even though David took Bathsheba as his wife after Uriah's death, she is listed in the genealogy of Christ, as "Uriah's wife" (Matthew 1:6).

She Repented and Received the Forgiveness of God

II Samuel 12:13 tells of David's repentance for the sin. It makes no sense to think that David, a man after God's own heart, would have continued to love and respect Bathsheba if she had not also repented and received the forgiveness of God.

She Received God's Unfailing Love

II Samuel 12:24-25 says, "Then David comforted Bathsheba his wife, and went in to her and lay with her. So she bore a son, and he called his name Solomon. Now the Lord loved him, and He sent word by the hand of Nathan the prophet: So he called him Jedidiah, because of the Lord."

This, indeed, is the unfailing love of God in action. Even the prophet, Nathan, who had pronounced God's judgment to David, named Solomon, Jedidiah, meaning "beloved of the Lord." Notice that the verse says it was "because of the Lord."

Was it because of any great deed that David or Bathsheba had done that the Lord placed His love on Solomon? No, it simply was the everlasting grace of God. His grace, His undeserved favor blessed David and Bathsheba with this beloved son.

What could you do to really impress the heart of this mighty God you serve? Fasting, good deeds or worship? What moves the very heart of God? Here is a contemporary example of the undeserved favor of God.

A friend of mine once had a vision of the throne room of heaven. God was sitting on His throne, and a crowd stood round with the seeming question of how they could best impress upon God their love and adoration for Him. As they spoke among themselves, the decision was made. Out stepped a very well known Christian singer. As she sang her highest notes with grace and poise, the crowd was amazed. Then Father God began to sing. He could sing higher and lower and with more vocal richness than the previous singer. The crowd stood in awe.

They began to talk among themselves again, and then sent a well-known trumpeter out to play a song of worship to the Lord. Once again the crowd was amazed at his abilities and thought that, surely, this would impress the Lord. Then the Lord reached down beside His throne, picked up a silver trumpet and began to play. As His trumpet hit the highest notes and played the most challenging composition, the crowd stood in awe once again.

They talked among themselves, almost in frustration as to what they should do. Then out from among them stepped a small boy, not very well dressed and not very impressive. He began to sing in a simple manner, "Jesus loves me, this I know . . ." As he sang, the crowd noticed a tear coming down the cheek of Father God. For you see, the one thing that impresses His heart the most is, very simply, the song of the redeemed. He cannot sing the song of the redeemed, for He is the Redeemer.

What will pick you up and place you back into the arms of your loving God when you stumble and fall? His love and His grace. The song of redemption carries within it the heart of repentance and trust and makes confession of the Father's absolute unconditional love. Yes, Solomon, or Jedidiah, was beloved of the Lord because of the Lord, not because of any good works his father or mother could do. So it will be with you. Your steps will be graced with the love of God simply because of who He is, not because of what you have or have not done. His mercy will pick you back up when you fall. Through this mercy, you will walk on and be effective.

She Responded in Faith

Bathsheba did not allow this sin to ruin her future. She had a choice, and she made it. I can imagine that she prayed Psalm 51:1-12 with David:

"Have mercy upon me, O God, according to your lovingkindness; according to the multitude of your tender mercies, blot out my transgressions. Wash me thoroughly from my iniquity, and cleanse me from my sin. For I acknowledge my transgressions, and my sin is always before me. Against you, you only, have I sinned and done this evil in your sight—that you may be found just when you speak, and blameless when you judge. Behold, I was brought forth in iniquity, and in sin my mother conceived me. Behold, you desire truth in the inward parts, and in the hidden part You will make me to know wisdom. Purge me with hyssop, and I shall be clean; wash me, and I shall be whiter than snow. Let me hear joy and gladness that the bones you have broken may rejoice. Hide your face from my sins, and blot out all my iniquities. Create in me a clean heart, O God, and renew a steadfast spirit within me. Do not cast me from your presence, and do not take your Holy Spirit from me. Restore to me the joy of Your salvation, and uphold me by Your generous Spirit."

Forgiveness is a powerful force in one's life when it is acted on with faith. However, brooding over sins that God has already forgiven will stifle your spiritual growth. This response would be sin because it contradicts God's act of forgiveness. It lacks wisdom, to say the least, and will rob you of spiritual progress and effectiveness in ministering to those around you.

Bathsheba did not brood. She returned to her covenant, her calling. She got up by God's grace and poured wisdom into her sons. She knew who was on her side.

She Imparted Her Wisdom to Others

Bathsheba was not perfect; yet she was used by God to fulfill His purposes. The fact that she retained influence on David until his death is proven in I Kings chapter one, when she reminded him of his promise to make Solomon his successor. Also in this instance, it is demonstrated that she had obviously won the respect of Nathan, the prophet. We also see that Solomon honored and respected his mother. He made her the Queen-mother, as she sat at his right hand (I Kings 2). Not only did she win the respect of the men in her life, but God also used her as a woman of wisdom and He allowed her to be mentioned throughout history in the lineage of Christ (Matthew 1:6).

Bathsheba had not only learned personally from her experience, but she also imparted her wisdom to others. Some Bible scholars suggest that she most likely composed portions of Proverbs thirty-one. She supposedly wrote this for Solomon when he was about to marry one of Pharaoh's daughters. Can you imagine what went through her mind as she wrote Proverbs 31:2-3, 10-12? "O my son, O son of my womb, O son of my vows, do not spend your strength on women, your vigor on those who ruin kings. . . . A wife of noble character who can find? She is worth far more than rubies. Her husband has full confidence in her and lacks nothing of value. . . " (NIV).

No, she could not stay at the feet of the enemy. She had to rise up, return to the covenant of her God and continue to run the race. The calling belonged to her, not to another. She was the one with the message of covenant to give to a generation. Through failure, that message had only become clearer and stronger within her. She was no slave to her failure; she made it work for her.

She Received a Blessing

Although Bathsheba sinned and paid the price for it, she was blessed with five sons. Her first son died, but her second son, Solomon, whose name means "peaceful, safe, well, happy and friendly," became a king and is forever in the lineage of Christ. Her third son was "Shimea." His name means "something heard." I think Bathsheba heard the good news–another son of blessing had come into her care. Her fourth son was Shobab, meaning "rebellious." As she had once been rebellious herself, I am sure she guided him with the hand of wisdom. Her fifth son was Nathan, meaning "given." This son must have been especially endeared to her, as she most likely named him after Nathan, the prophet. She and the old prophet must have become close friends as the grace of God was bestowed on their history together. What treasures and signs of God's everlasting love these sons must have been to this mother of grace and wisdom!

What Can I Learn from Bathsheba's Example?

Let Bathsheba's failure warn you that you must be on guard continually, and do not think that you are above falling because you have a spiritual heritage. As J.B. Phillips wrote, "God has no grandchildren, only sons and daughters." A Christian heritage is a blessing and strength, but it is not a guarantee. We each must walk our own journey before the Lord and serve Him faithfully.

As with Bathsheba, temptation in its various forms may knock at your door one day, but never let failure come in and abide. If failure does step foot inside your door, do not let it stay. Allow the Lord to change it into good by making it work for you. By doing so, you walk in His amazing grace and enabling anointing. Romans 8:28 so gloriously says, "And we know that all things work together for good to those who love God, to those who are the called according to His purpose." Everything that comes your way and every response that comes out of your heart will not be good, but you can make these situations work for good for you and the people you serve.

Verse twenty-nine of Romans eight follows with, "For whom He foreknew, He also predestined to be conformed to the image of his Son..."

The goal in all that you do should be to please Him and to become like Him. When failure comes, allow His unfailing, unconditional love to conform you into the likeness of Jesus.

Like Bathsheba, be reconciled to God, and do not allow your failure to ruin your tomorrow. Accept your imperfection, stay alert and on guard and allow God to fulfill His purposes in and through you. Then, put the enemy to flight by imparting wisdom to the next generation.

If you are reading this as one who has fallen and are struggling with reconciling yourself to God's continued desire to work through you, please receive the following words from the Master.

Scriptures Of Encouragement (NIV)

". . . I have loved you with an everlasting love; I have drawn you with lovingkindness. I will build you up again and you will be rebuilt . . ." (Jeremiah 31:3-4).

"Nevertheless, I will bring health and healing to it; I will heal my people and will let them enjoy abundant peace and security" (Jeremiah 33:6).

"And you will know the truth, and the truth will set you free" (John 8:32).

"You are already clean because of the word I have spoken to you. Remain in me, and I will remain in you. No branch can bear fruit by itself; it must remain in the vine. Neither can you bear fruit unless you remain in me" (John 15:3-4).

"Therefore, there is now no condemnation for those who are in Christ Jesus, because through Christ Jesus the law of the Spirit of life set me free from the law of sin and death" (Romans 8:1-2).

"And that is what some of you were. But you were washed, you were sanctified, you were justified in the name of the Lord Jesus Christ and by the Spirit of our God" (I Corinthians 6:11).

"Therefore, if anyone is in Christ, he is a new creation; and the old has gone, the new has come!" (II Corinthians 5:17).

"And be made new in the attitude of your minds; and to put on the new self, created to be like God in true righteousness and holiness" (Ephesians 4:23-24).

"Being confident of this, that he who began a good work in you will carry it on to completion until the day of Christ Jesus" (Philippians 1:6).

"Let us draw near to God with a sincere heart in full assurance of faith, having our hearts sprinkled to cleanse us from a guilty conscience and having our bodies washed with pure water. Let us hold unswervingly to the hope we profess, for he who promised is faithful" (Hebrews 10:22-23).

". . . you have purified yourselves by obeying the truth . . ." (I Peter 1:22).

"He has showed you what is good. And what does the Lord require of you? To act justly and to love mercy and to walk humbly with your God" (Micah 6:8).

"Do not gloat over me, my enemy! Though I have fallen, I will rise. Though I sit in darkness, the Lord will be my light" (Micah 7:8).

SECTION TWO:

❈

your
Service

Chapter 6

HOME
A Keeper of the Home

"**I'M** taking a 'sick day' off from work today. I just can't handle it anymore. Every day I get up, go to work and come home to work. I get up, toss a load of clothes in the washing machine, make lunches for the kids and forgive myself for yet one more morning of not exercising because I chose to sleep in. I go to work to meet the demands of my boss and to earn the extra money that never seems to be there. I come home to clean up the dog's daily mess, put another load of clothes in the washer and then begin to boil water on the kitchen stove to give the illusion of cooking dinner. Then after dinner, I help the kids with homework, fold clothes and flop down on the couch, only to notice the forever fingerprints on the wall that really need to be washed off. I love my family, but I'm tired of being in demand. So here I sit with my coffee cup in hand, without a care. Lord, please, just for today, help me not hear the voices of demand and not see the never-ending tasks of homemaking." Have you ever written anything like this in your journal?

If not, perhaps your journal entry might read like this. "I'm taking a 'sick day' off from work today. I just can't handle it anymore. Every day I get up, go to work and come home to work. (Sound familiar?) It seems like my whole life is work. Everyone thinks I have so much free time just because I'm single, but I don't. After all, married women have help. They have their husbands and children to help with all of these chores. I love my singleness, Lord, but couldn't you please send me a little help with my homemaking 'to do' lists?"

Consider this journal entry. "I see the single gal across the street and the working mom next door are both taking days off today, Lord. When is my day off? These little ones around my legs making constant demands are adorable but exhausting. This 'in home' business is great to work at in between the demands of the children, but it's so hard to focus. The house seems to be continually exposing an unfinished project here or there. My office is not something that I 'go to' or 'get away from.' It forever surrounds me. I'm a 'keeper at home,' all right. I'm also trapped at home. I love my little ones and my home business, Lord, but please help me to focus on one and not be distracted by the other, so as to keep my sanity intact."

Can you relate to any of these thoughts? What about the never-ending tasks of homemaking, the "to do" lists and the office that you can never get away from?

Is the Scriptural Advice on Homemaking Relevant to Me?

In Titus chapter two, Paul tells Titus to teach the older women to "be reverent in behavior . . ." and too, in turn, teach the younger women to be "homemakers." The King James Version says "keepers at home," and the New International Version says, "be busy at home."

He indirectly expresses an admonition to the young, married women. In this context, he is emphasizing the importance of loving their husbands and children and being pure and kind. In I Timothy 5:13-14, Paul even speaks concern for the young widows in Ephesus who had gotten into the habit of being "idle, wandering about from house to house, and not only idle but also gossips and busy bodies, saying things which they ought not." Paul's solution for this is that they ". . . marry, bear children, manage the house . . ."

In a day when the philosophy of egalitarianism and women's liberation has penetrated and influenced the thinking of both men and women,

Paul's admonition in these passages often arouses a variety of emotional responses. Interpretations, questions and accusations are strong and varied toward the apostle who also proclaimed ". . . there is neither male nor female; for you are all one in Christ Jesus" (Galatians 3:28).

Some say Paul has limited his writing here to his Jewish culture and the era in which he lived. To adhere to this philosophy causes some serious hermeneutical problems for the reader. It could, in fact, raise questions regarding the inspiration and authority of the Bible. If Paul was in error in this portion of Scripture, what about other portions of Scripture in which he explains how salvation comes to each of us? (By the way, his reference in Galatians three, "neither male nor female," refers to salvation, not function.)

Personally, I believe that Paul was writing all of his books under the inspiration of the Holy Spirit. I believe implicitly in the authority of the Bible as the Word of God. Many portions of Scripture, written in various cultural settings, do have to be interpreted and applied to our present culture and generation appropriately, but all do apply.

I do not believe that Paul is saying that women are to be limited to managing a household. That would deny all that Proverbs thirty-one says of the virtuous woman, who was a very fruitful businesswoman and praised by her family. Paul is not limiting women. He is simply acknowledging that being a keeper (Titus 2:5) or a manager (I Timothy 5:14) of the home is meant to be a part of the call.

What is My Role Within the Home?

Statistics given in contemporary magazines, news journals and television programming tell us that, even though women are "liberated" today, they are still doing most of the household work. In fact, many say that they are doing eighty percent of the work around the house.

I don't mean to imply, by the Scriptures just given, that men should not contribute more significantly to work in the home. I believe that, in the busy, contemporary family, they definitely should. However, how they contribute will vary from household to household. It is interesting to note that numerous pollsters report that men who are in traditional marriages do more work around the house than men who claim to be in marriages of equality.

We must come to grips with the fact that there is a difference between partnership and equality. As Galatians says, we are all equal in Christ. However, within the context of partnership, we may each function in such a way as to complement the other. The wife has been given the mandate to be a keeper or manager of the home. However, the husband has been given the mandate to love his wife as Christ loved the church (Philippians 2; I Peter 3). The man, who obeys this mandate and loves his wife unselfishly, may find himself willingly busying himself in household chores. Equally true, the wife, who obeys her biblical mandate, may also find herself willingly entrenched in doing or delegating household chores as well.

Although homemaking is for both the single and the married woman, Christians as well as non-Christians have often been guilty of mis-defining a married woman's role in regard to homemaking. The traditional marital concept of role delegation, male employment and female homemaking, does not necessarily equate with the biblical concept of marriage and homemaking. We need to be careful to honor biblical principles above traditions, rather than generational traditions above true biblical principles.

The roles that worked for the average family four decades ago may not necessarily work for the family today. However, a roleless marriage, as some would suggest, will not work either. For marriage and home management to work today, there must be complementing partnership. This, in fact, simply means that each partner must be willing to function in a variety of roles at different times and seasons.

One of the biggest mistakes women make is comparing themselves among themselves (II Corinthians 10:12). This mistake usually kills any grace that is in operation. We must allow each other to function in our homemaking roles as is best suited to us individually, as long as it flows within the biblical context. In other words, as long as a husband and wife are submitting to one another in the love of Christ (Ephesians 5), it doesn't really matter who washes the dishes, the husband, the wife or the dishwasher. This same principle would apply for singles and other house-partners (i.e., siblings, roommates, etc.) as well.

In the context of marriage, whether a husband helps out or not, his wife should not deny her part in practical homemaking, simply to avoid doing something demeaning or boring. Every job has some menial or boring aspect to it. For the teacher, it may be grading papers. For the nurse, it may be bedpan duty. For the pianist, it may be practicing scales. When these mundane parts of a job are woven into the fabric of the whole, even they can become fulfilling and meaningful. If managing the home is part of the calling, can we not expect an anointing of grace and joy to go with this part of the call, as much as with any other facet?

How Is Keeping the Home a Part of My Ministry Calling?

Caring for your physical home will minister volumes to your family and guests. A well-ordered home potentially affects your friends, molds your marriage and shapes your children. Proverbs 14:1 says, "The wise woman builds her house, but the foolish pulls it down with her hands." If your family lives in constant clutter and an unkempt atmosphere, they may struggle with feelings of insecurity and anxiousness. Lack of proper nutrition, clothing that is wrinkled and unclean, a home that is dirty and uninviting communicates to those with whom you live that they are not important enough to have "a prepared place."

When they read in God's Word that He has a prepared place, they may wonder what exactly His definition of a prepared place is, if they have rarely experienced one. When He tells them to "be anxious for nothing," their souls may cry out, "Are you kidding?! I always have to worry. I never know if there's going to be any clean socks, ironed shirts or anything for my lunch. I'm not even sure if I'll be embarrassed or not when a friend comes over unexpectedly."

Family members are not generally embarrassed by a lack of expensive clothes, exquisite homes or gourmet meals. However, they are easily humiliated if the simplest of their surroundings or possessions are not clean and in order. No outside involvement is so important that your home should be in constant disarray. I'm not talking about perfection. I'm speaking of constant disarray.

Many years ago, when marriage was on the near horizon for me, I spoke with the mother of a friend of mine. She gave me permission to tell her story whenever it would benefit anyone. She was a woman who had many wonderful leadership skills and gifts to offer the Body of Christ. One night, at a time when she had been asking the Lord what her job assignment from Him might be, she had a dream. In the dream she saw herself teaching a group of people the Word of God. After awaking from this dream, she determined that she would find an effective place of ministry in the church. She went from one class to another, from one Bible study group to another, from one church to another, busily offering her services and looking for that place of perfect fulfillment and ministry.

After many years of busyness and frustration, never feeling that she had quite found a place of ministry fulfillment, she began to seek the Lord again about her ministry. One particular night, as she put her head on her pillow, she had the same dream that she had had many years before. She could see herself teaching ever so effectively. However, this time she saw the faces of the people who she was teaching. They were the faces of her five sons. Much to her horror, she awakened in grief, realizing that she had so busied herself, looking for her place of ministry in the church, that she had neglected the needs of her children and their spiritual education at her knee. At the time that she told me her story, only one of her five adult sons was serving the Lord. She was in deep regret.

Whether you are married with children or single, you will affect the next generation by your example in this area. One of my very close friends is a single woman. She has made her home enjoyable, not only for herself and her adult friends, but also for her nephews and niece. My children enjoyed being in her warm and well-kept home a number of times as they were growing up. She is still endeared to their hearts even as adults today. Her home is always a prepared place for her guests, big or small. She is effectively shaping the next generation, through her gift of singleness, in her home and out of her home.

We must be so careful to be keepers of the home. In so doing, we will carefully shape a generation. That shaping may be unseen to our natural eyes, but it will be indelibly imprinted onto the hearts of those we love the most.

Is There a Spiritual Application to the Practical Nature of Keeping the Home?

Another aspect of being a keeper of the home is revealed through a spiritual insight. The woman in Proverbs thirty-one did literally get up in the early morning hours and prepare breakfast for her family and maidservants, but she did much more than that.

"Night" in this verse means that she got up in the middle of her own personal adversity, perhaps even in the middle of her own hormonal confusion, and prepared a good spiritual word for her family and all of those with whom she would come in contact that day. In other words, she loved those of her household enough to rise above her own emotional lows, speak the Word of the Lord to them and send them off into their day with words of encouragement and praise. She knew how to get beyond herself and her concerns and minister to others. This not to say that she never took care of her own emotional needs or never let anyone else minister to her, but she did know how to rise up and give out, even when she was down–and so must you. Woman, you are called and anointed! You can do it!

A widow once told me, "Life is what you have, not what you wished you had." Your life circumstances are not always going to go as planned. Even with the best-made plans, there will be times when the house will not get cleaned and the laundry will not get done. Groceries may not even get purchased, much less dinner cooked! The whole "keeper at home" phrase will grate against you. When you begin to feel this pull, the enemy is fast at work. Don't let him get you down.

I like what Paul says in II Corinthians 6:3-10, "Don't put it off; don't frustrate God's work by showing up late, throwing a question mark over everything we're doing. Our work as God's servants gets validated-or not-in the details. People are watching us as we stay at our post, alertly, unswervingly . . . in hard times, tough times, bad times; when we're beaten up, jailed, and mobbed; working hard, working late, working without eating; with pure heart, clear head, steady hand; in gentleness, holiness, and honest love; when we're telling the truth, and when God's showing his power; when we're doing our best setting things right; when we're praised, and when we're blamed; slandered, and honored; true to our word, though distrusted; ignored by the world, but recognized by God; terrifically alive, though rumored to be dead; beaten within an inch of our lives, but refusing to die; immersed in tears, yet always filled with deep joy; living on handouts, yet enriching many; having nothing, having it all" (The Message).

Let the Lord open your eyes daily to see the spiritual in the natural and the eternal in the moment.

What if I Can't Do It All Alone?

The journal illustrations, given at the beginning of this chapter, primarily reflect women who are frustrated and tired with the loads they are carrying, at least for the moment. What they do not reflect are the moments experienced in the fulfillment of a task completed, a peaceful atmosphere or a thankful family. What they also do not reflect are the discovered moments of amazing sanity as towels are being folded, the endorphins that are released while vacuuming or the joy of training and delegating practical life skills to others.

The most effective way I know to walk in peace and joy in managing a household is to realize that I cannot do it all alone. If you have not already come to this realization, then stop and take a deep look at everything and everyone around you. As you do, you may begin to see some area that has been overlooked while you have been single-handedly attempting to do it all.

This area of oversight may be your own health, your relationships, or the nutrition on your dinner table. It may be your personal time in the presence of the Lord, your laundry or maybe something else. I guarantee that if you look closely, you will discover that you cannot do it all by yourself for very many years. If you've been trying to, stop now!

Stop and assess what area of your life may be suffering, and ask if it's worthwhile for that area or that relationship to miss out on your personal attention. Then ask yourself if there is something on your agenda that could be delegated to your family members, your friends or others. These others may not accomplish the task with the same expertise that you do, but does that really matter to the eternal purposes of God? Perhaps, it really only matters to you—to your own pride. (Oops! Sorry, didn't mean to step on any toes. Mine have been flattened with this realization a few times too!)

Take a second look at Proverbs 31:15. Do you see the phrase, "and a portion to her maidservants?" How did this virtuous woman have time to prepare breakfast and devotions? She had maidservants! Now, for those of you who have ever had maidservants, you know that you need to have a prepared Scripture on hand to give them in order to motivate them to serve effectively. For those of you who have never come close to having a maidservant, washers, dryers, dishwashers and vacuum cleaners are your maidservants. The problem is that these machines do not run totally on their own. They like to be emptied regularly, serviced occasionally and spoken to with terms of endearment. Most of all, they like to be used.

As a Christian woman who is called to be an influence, be a self-starter, and be motivated to work on your own without being coaxed into it. Simply be responsible for keeping your home clean and prepared to receive family members and guests. Generally speaking, people do not consider piles of dirty laundry or strewn about, day-old pizza boxes to be conversational atmosphere.

This sounds strong, I know, but keeping your home clean and in order does not necessarily mean that you have to do it all single-handedly. It simply means that you are responsible to make sure that it gets done. If you work from within your home and your schedule is flexible, this may mean that you have the time to do your own cleaning. If you work full-time outside of the home, you may not be able to keep your house clean and do everything else that is required of you. Ask the Lord and those who live with you, where they desire for you to place your priorities. Face it–you really cannot do it all alone!

Simply put, getting the work done is being a good steward of that which God has blessed you with. Jesus did a lot of teaching about stewardship while He walked the earth. Whether stewardship means doing dishes or shopping for groceries, we need to be good stewards. However, this does not mean that we have to do it all alone.

Have you ever wondered how Abigail was able to put together all of those food provisions for David and his men so quickly and efficiently? She had maidens too! Abigail couldn't do it all alone, and the virtuous wife in Proverbs thirty-one, who received great praise from her husband and children, couldn't do it all alone either. Both Abigail and our Proverbs thirty-one woman were efficient keepers of the home by being good home managers.

If neither Abigail nor the "virtuous woman" could do it all alone in Old Testament days, when the pace was slower and the tasks at hand were pretty constant, perhaps you should give yourself a little space in the busyness of this constantly changing, contemporary age. Again, the point is not how the work gets done, but simply that it gets done. The heart of a woman, who loves her home and her family, will see to it that the home affairs are managed well. This goes for the single woman, as well as the married woman.

A wise woman, who is called and anointed by God, does not do it all alone! She delegates! If you do try to do it all, there may be nagging, little voices that will begin to haunt your thoughts. You may begin to hears things like these:

"I'm tired and it's their fault."

Shifting the blame to others usually comes first when you are tired or when you've been hurt. People will happily let you do all the work if you convince them by your actions that you can do it all on your own. They will have fun, relax and enhance their own personal growth while you keep working. When you get tired, you'll be tempted to blame them for your tiredness. If the job was never delegated, the ball was never tossed, so to speak, how would they know? They will go through life ignorant and happy, and you will pass through it bitter and tired. This definitely is not a pretty picture for a Christian woman who is called to be an example to others.

"Scream!"

This is an all-time favorite of stress counselors. Primal scream therapy is one way that contemporary therapists try to loosen people up. You can scream, pound the floor, throw an egg with your family members' names on it, and you will still only find temporary relief. Screaming, with intent to hurt or belittle a person into taking responsibility, is hurtful and ineffective, at best. It also shifts the blame from the root to the plant and confuses the real area of need.

"Live for yourself."

This little voice says, "Take the phone off the hook. Don't shop, cook or clean anymore. Go on a crying binge, a food binge, a spending binge-some binge, any binge-just focus on you. Be sure that you absolutely refuse to reach out to others until your needs get met." Wow! At this point, you'll even amaze yourself at how ungodly you can be.

When you feel weary and taken advantage of, you'll tend to make choices out of a posture of weariness, rather than out of grace.

"Give up–quit!"

This little voice continues, "Quit the job. Quit the ministry. Quit the marriage!" At this point you feel ambivalent, trapped. You have let the burden of details completely defuse your victorious stance in Christ. As Song of Solomon 2:15 says, it is "...the little foxes that spoil the vines..."

Our calling in this area is, truly, to home management. This may involve actually busying yourself with practical chores within the home, or it may mean that you train or pay others to do it. The point is not so much that you do every chore, but rather that you see to it that it gets done.

How Can I Balance All These Areas of My Life?

You must remember that being a keeper of the home has everything to do with shaping and training the next generation. It is not just a matter of pushing a broom and cooking a roast for Sunday dinner. It is molding a generation to follow on behind. Again, single or married, we are all responsible to effectively touch the next generation in a positive way.

A poem by an unknown author says it this way:
I took a piece of plastic clay and idly fashioned it one day.
As my fingers pressed it still, it bent and yielded to my will.
I came again when days were past. The bit of clay was hard at last.
My early impress still it bore, and I could change its form no more.

You take a piece of living clay, and gently form it day by day.
Molding with your power and art, a young boy's soft and yielding heart.
You come again when years are gone; it is a man you look upon.
Your early impress still he bore; and you can change him never more."

The key to balancing time between people and home responsibilities is not to separate the two. View keeping the home as part of your ministry to others; and part of your ministry to others as keeping the home. Sometimes the most therapeutic thing I can do for myself is to go home, vacuum, dust or clean out a closet. When I have my house in order, I am more at peace with myself and with others. It is funny how that works. Getting my natural house in order uniquely blesses and benefits my spiritual house. If things are in order at home, I don't feel pressured to end fellowship times with others quickly. The pressure is off!

I am so thankful to have learned most of what I needed to know about balancing a very full schedule from my very wise and godly mother. She has always been a wonderful keeper of the home. She didn't have the privilege of being a stay-at-home mom. She worked a full-time job outside of the home from the time that I went to kindergarten until I went to college. She kept the house clean, nutritious meals on the table, laundry ironed and folded, cupcakes ready for endless class parties and a smile on her face. She even found time to help with school homework!

What was even more impressive, she always looked nice. Oh yes, I saw her in curlers, but she actually brushed her hair and put on lipstick on a regular basis. I was very proud of her. I really thought she was quite beautiful. She was amazingly efficient in so many ways!

I remember learning responsibility, as each family member had chores. I learned everything from being a "super-duper-pooper-scooper" for our pet dog to vacuuming, dusting, baking cookies and boiling wieners. However, I never remember feeling that she was too consumed with her concerns to stop and train me in how to do these various and sundry chores. Neither do I remember feeling that I couldn't measure up to her standard. She was quick to give me a "job-well-done" encouragement. I knew she cared about me personally, so I was motivated to do my part in order that the whole family would function well together.

Is that not good training for being a woman of influence in the Body of Christ today?! Think of it—each member doing his or her part out of a motivation of love and commitment to the family. Of course, this can only happen if there is disciplined, loving mentoring.

So what is the practical hope that I learned from my mother? What is a reasonable response to balancing ministry and being an efficient and joyful keeper of the home? There are three basic things that have helped me over the years.

Get Sufficient Rest

Psalm 127:2 says, "It is vain for you to rise up early, to sit up late, to eat the bread of sorrows; for so He gives His beloved sleep." You need to get sufficient rest. Become aware of your own biological time clock. Some people can get by on five or six hours of sleep; some need eight to ten hours. The majority of us need six to eight hours of sleep at night. Yes, there will be times when you can stretch your body to the limits. However, when you do this, you will need to plan some extra time of rest and refreshing.

There is a reason that God ordered the calendar with a day of Sabbath rest in mind. Your body needs a regular, consistent day of rest, especially if you're not getting enough rest during the week. If you don't learn to rest your body on a consistent basis when you are young, you'll pay for it with your health later in life. It will catch up with you. So, listen to your body.

I am not suggesting laziness, here. You were designed to work. Work brings great fulfillment. There may even be times when you will need to override emotional or physical tiredness to push through a project, appointment or church service leaning completely on the strength of Christ. Effectiveness and rest go together like paint on wood–rest enhances flexibility, strength and fulfillment of purpose. Work hard, but get appropriate rest.

Maintain Proper Nutrition and Consistent Exercise

Nurturing your body with healthy food and exercise will pay off daily and in the long run. Exercise and proper nutrition are stress-reducers for your daily, busy lifestyle. That is considerably important when you are called to work closely with people.

God chose to make our bodies His localized residence, and we should be good stewards of that property. I Corinthians 6:19 says, ". . . do you not know that your body is the temple of the Holy Spirit who is in you, whom you have from God, and you are not your own?" There are over seven hundred and fifty Scripture verses in the four Gospels that deal with miracles relating to the physical, natural body of mankind. This means that approximately twenty percent of the verses found in the Gospels deal with the subject of the human body. I think that God cares about our bodies. If He does, then we should also. In talking with numerous women over the years, I know that physical exercise and proper nutrition are perhaps the most common areas that we overlook when we're busy taking care of everyone else. It is easy not to make time for ourselves. Easy, but not wise.

Organize Your Time

A great deal of stress can be alleviated through an efficient, organized lifestyle. Accept the fact that you will probably never be totally organized. People's needs tend to disrupt even the best-organized plans. However, a tentative plan and basic order in your surroundings can help immensely. The remaining stress is relieved through trust in God and the ability to be flexible, available and adjustable. For time management to begin to relieve pressure you will need to have a very strong realization of the truth that ". . . all discipline for the moment seems not to be joyful, but sorrowful; yet to those who have been trained by it, afterwards it yields the peaceful fruit of righteousness" (Hebrews 12:11). The discipline of consistent order and scheduling can be quite freeing. However, if the schedule has you, rather than you having the schedule, you could end up in bondage. Simply said, make a plan, and then give that plan to God. Let me add a few practical tips here:

Value the Minute

Minutes make up life. Do not waste five-minute segments of time. See what you can accomplish in just a few minutes. You will probably amaze yourself.

Learn to Delegate Authority

Others will never learn to be efficient and sharp in their gifts if you do not release them to do it. Perhaps the task will not be done exactly the way that you would have liked it done, but at least it's done. The early stages of delegation can cost more time in training, but in the long run, delegation multiplies your effectiveness.

When my daughter was young, I taught her how to bake chocolate chip cookies. Initially, it took more time to teach her than it would have taken if I had been doing it alone. However, after a few good lessons, she became the best cookie-baker in the house. I no longer needed to give my time to that task as long as she was around.

The same principle applies when training others, staffing a team effort or administrating a program. To delegate means to release others and multiply yourself. As a Christian mentor and discipler, part of your job is to equip and release others to minister. You are actually fulfilling the work of Christ when you train and delegate.

Eliminate Unnecessary Tasks–Simplify!

This is an amazingly simple, yet frequently overlooked suggestion. It is as simple as this list:

(1) Purchase yearly birthday cards for all extended family members at the same time.
(2) Have an on-going shopping list for the family or those who live with you. Encourage them to add to it as they have needs (i.e., tooth paste, light bulbs, etc.).
(3) Educate the family to eat in the kitchen or dining room rather than all over the house.
(4) Purchase "no-iron" tablecloths.

The list could go on and on, but I'm sure that you understand the point.

Make the Telephone Your Co-Partner

Have a message center by the phone that includes a monthly calendar, a need-to-know phone list and an erasable message board. Do telephone research to compare prices and check on the availability of items before hopping into your car to shop. Before visiting someone who is hospitalized, telephone to make sure that the patient is still in the hospital and is able to have visitors. If you do not telephone ahead, you may arrive, only to find that he or she has already checked out or has a "no visitors" sign on the door.

Organize Your House

Evaluate each room for its best functional use. All items should either add to the decorative or functional purpose of the room. Get rid of the clutter! Clutter should be public enemy number one in your household. Look for trouble spots in each room, determine the cause and fix the problem. If you are a mother, realize that most children need a clutter drawer or treasure box for their Sunday school papers, projects, etc. Don't be such a perfectionist that your family members are not allowed to have a corner or box that is all theirs. (After all, you may want a corner yourself.) Divide your clutter into three piles–throw away, give away and put away. This is a good rule to follow while sorting: if you will not need it within a year, get rid of it.

Create a Filing System That Works for You

Most people need a filing system. My filing system includes everything from warrantees and guarantees to biblical character studies. Computers are wonderful for storing important information, but it is wise to keep a hard copy of numerous items of important research and study.

Having a file to record where you have put certain items that you rarely use can be helpful also. In those moments of hormonal overload when all the brain circuits are down, this little file is a sure blessing.

In your computer or your manual filing system, it is beneficial to keep a file on practical preferences of visiting guests. Knowing if a guest prefers chicken to beef, chocolate to fruit or a firm mattress to a soft mattress is helpful. Your hospitality notoriety will go up if your guests think that you actually remembered their preferences from their previous visit five years ago!

Have a "Noteworthy" Notebook

The Lord, your family, friends and co-workers constantly love to have your listening ear. When you are continually flooded with data on everything from business decisions to picking up your child from the first grade parking lot, giving a listening ear and remembering what was actually said are sometimes two different issues. Keeping a notebook nearby is often a great time saver. Your notebook should be orderly, multi-purpose and it should reflect your daily life.

"Noteworthy" notebooks are not for show. The purpose is not to impress anyone with how important or how busy you are. This notebook should simply to be a tool in your hands to make your life less stressful.

If you have never used a notebook, a few suggested items to include might be phone numbers, addresses, family sizes and gift ideas, price comparisons, "to do" lists, sermon notes, thoughts from the Lord, quotes and calendars. Again, what you might put in your notebook depends on you and your daily needs. I call my notebook my "paper brain." It stays close by my side and helps to order my day and my memory.

How Will the Lord Help Me?

Most of the time, it is best to put yourself in neutral gear and just let the Lord do the driving. He has the master plan. He is the only One who really knows what is most important to do and when to do it. The only way that you will be able to rise ". . . while it is yet night . . ." is to discern the Master's plan and walk in it (Proverbs 31:15).

Whether you hire someone to clean your house and shop for your groceries or you do it yourself, the important thing is your stewardship of what God has given you. Resist the temptation to do it all on your own. Stewardship of the home goes beyond the natural home and the natural groceries. It extends to your natural family and your church family. Include others. Be bold. Be vulnerable. Shape the next generation to also be keepers of the home.

Chapter 7

HOSPITALITY
A Woman of Servanthood

Living in such an egalitarian-prone society, we can become easily intimidated and not claim certain privileges of Christian servanthood. Hospitality is a privilege that our society often reduces to a gender role debate. Rather than focusing on the varied benefits and grace that flow easily from womanhood, society wants to restrain women by guilt association from enjoying God-given leadership privileges in this area. We need to let God help us reclaim the beauty and grace of the ministry of hospitality.

Is Hospitality Part of My Calling?

Only a few women have leadership roles with a public expression, such as preaching, teaching, administrating or worship leading. However, every woman has a home out of which the ministry of hospitality can flow. Hospitality is, in fact, a requirement of ministerial leadership in the Body of Christ.

Whether you are single or married, poor or rich, you have something to offer someone else through your hospitality. When others have opened their homes to me, I have been served gourmet meals, as well as the simplest morsels. I myself have spent many hours and many dollars in preparation for some meals offered at my table in hospitality, and I have, at other times, offered popcorn on napkins and water in glasses. Regardless of the preparation and expense, what always shines through most is the preparation and richness of the heart that is offered.

As Christian believers, hospitality is most certainly part of our calling. The Bible clearly charges all of God's servants to be hospitable. Consider these verses.

"Share with God's people who are in need. Practice hospitality" (Romans 12:13, NIV).

"Now the overseer must be above reproach, the husband of but one wife, temperate, self-controlled, respectable, hospitable, able to teach . . ." (I Timothy 3:2, NIV).

"Rather he must be hospitable, one who loves what is good, who is self-controlled, upright, holy and disciplined" (Titus 1:8, NIV).

"Do not forget to entertain strangers, for by so doing some people have entertained angels without knowing it" (Hebrews 13:2, NIV).

"Offer hospitality to one another without grumbling" (I Peter 4:9, NIV).

"The King will reply, 'I tell you the truth, whatever you did for one of the least of these brothers of mine, you did for me' " (Matthew 25:40, NIV).

What are Some Biblical Examples of Hospitality?

There are many examples of hospitality in the Bible. Think about the examples that follow.

Genesis 18:1-8

I call this "Sarah's siesta." Three heavenly visitors came to visit Abraham and Sarah. They arrived in the heat of day, during Sarah's rest time. Instead of continuing to allow herself her well-deserved siesta, she got up and ministered to the uninvited guests.

Sometimes your guests will come uninvited by you, but they will have been invited by the Lord. At these times, be careful to discern the Lord's intention before giving them your appointment schedule or turning them away abruptly.

Genesis 24:18-20

These verses describe "Rebekah's refreshing." Rebekah was obviously a young woman who carried the spirit of hospitality within her heart, regardless of where she was. She was busy attending to her daily business at the well, and a stranger suddenly approached her and asked for a drink. Immediately, she offered him a drink and then offered to water his camels as well. This would have been quite an effort that went beyond the normal extension of hospitality.

In ancient cultures, wells usually had a flight of stairs that went down to the water, so that the women could easily dip in their pitchers. The pitchers were made of earthenware, not plasticware. In other words, the pitchers were not very light even before they were filled with water.

Think of Rebekah going up and down a flight of stairs several times with a full earthenware pitcher of water to fill a trough for several camels (which could each drink enough water for several days). Now that's hospitality! I might pump gasoline for a few cars, but I don't know how motivated I would be to pump fuel for several semi-trucks, especially if I had to run up and down a flight of stairs to do it. How about you?!

Joshua 2:1-16

This could appropriately be called "Rahab's risk." Sometimes hospitality is costly in more ways than one. Rahab risked her life and the lives of her family members to offer shelter to these two spies.

There will be times when your own reputation may be at stake as you are led of the Lord to offer certain individuals hospitality. It's amazing that many people fall into the habit of offering hospitality only to those who can repay it. Let yourself be stirred afresh to consider offering hospitality to those who cannot give anything in return.

II Samuel 9:7-13

I call this "David's devotion." Sometimes hospitality may need to extend beyond one generation and be offered to those who cannot repay it. Mephibosheth, the handicapped son of Jonathan and grandson of Saul, was doomed to a life of poverty and seclusion. David's hand of hospitality was overwhelmingly generous to this young man. David reached to him out of a heart of devotion to his friend Jonathan.

When you are young, your parents may have friends who will need hospitality. When you are older, your children may have friends who will need hospitality. Be open to whomever the Lord brings your way. Let blessing pass from one generation to the next, regardless of the lot and position of those in need.

I Kings 17:10-15 and II Kings 4:8-37; 8:1-6

In Kings, there are two examples, one of a woman who had little and one of a woman who had much. I Kings 17:10-15 shows us "the widow at Zarephath's zero." This poor widow had barely anything to offer, but she sacrificially gave to meet the needs of the prophet. In so doing, her faith was stirred to believe that her son's life, as well as her own, would be sustained. In II Kings 4:8-37 and 8:1-6, we see the "Shunammite's shine." This married woman served the prophet out of her natural abundance and spiritual need. She was wealthy but had no child to nurture. Both women had desires and needs. Both gave sacrificially to the prophet of God.

Sometimes you will rise up in your own "night" season and minister to others who are passing through. Sacrificial service will be your garment, and the Lord's provision will be your reward.

New Testament Examples

There are so many examples of hospitality in the Bible that books have been written on this topic alone. New Testament examples of this ministry are the sisters, Mary and Martha; Lydia, the rich woman; and Priscilla, who was in business with her husband. Other examples of those who ministered to Jesus directly were Simon, the leper, in Mark 14; Zacchaeus in Luke 19; and the country gentlemen on the road to Emmaus in Luke 24. The examples are so numerous that surely the Lord means for each of us to be involved in some way in this area.

What is the Purpose of Christian Hospitality?

The primary purpose of hospitality should be that the heart of Christ might be demonstrated in some practical expression of grace to those for whom He died. Whether this is through an elaborate meal or a cup of tea, the message should be one of grace and kindness to those who are lost or to those who have come to acknowledge Him as King. Romans 14:17-18 says, "For the kingdom of God is not a matter eating and drinking, but of righteousness, peace and joy in the Holy Spirit, because anyone who serves Christ in this way is pleasing to God and approved by men" (NIV).

Your table of hospitality should be a place of refuge for the weary of heart, whether they are family, friends or those who walk without knowledge of the Lord. Paul expressed the key well in Philippians 2:2-4, when he admonished, " . . . make my joy complete by being like-minded, having the same love, being one in spirit and purpose. Do nothing out of selfish ambition or vain conceit, but in humility consider others better then yourselves. Each of you should look not only to your own interests, but also to the interests of others" (NIV). As we follow Paul's advice, we will find our tables rarely empty and our hearts full.

How Can I Be Prepared to Entertain?

One key that may spark your interest in offering hospitality more often is to not do it all alone. Divide the practical work among friends and family members. Give everybody a specific area for which to be responsible, and watch the fun begin. If you can allow things to be imperfect, you can also relax and enjoy the benefits of teamwork. In teamwork, things may not be as perfect as you would like them, but if you can let that go and focus on your part, you will enjoy it more. If you delegate effectively, some areas may be better than if you did them yourself. Do not let comparison get hold of you. Enjoy what each person has to offer. As much of hospitality is simply a practical expression of love and wisdom in action, please allow me to offer a few foundational tips.

Be Prepared

Make your bed as soon as your feet hit the floor in the morning, and clean up the kitchen right after breakfast. When cleaning your house, do so room by room, in the order that one would progressively see the rooms after entering the front door.

Place items that reflect you and your family around the home within view. They will invite conversation and interaction. A few suggestions would be family pictures, collectibles or personal artwork.

Have something on hand for visiting children, such as crayons, coloring books, children's reading books, toy cars, special place mats, cups and plates, etc.

Be Flexible

If pre-planning is not possible, it is important to be flexible. Instant entertaining is a part of the ministry; learn to enjoy it. Do away with any pride and perfectionist tendencies in this area.

Enjoy Yourself

Be sure that you are having a good time when you have guests. If you are enjoying yourself, then your guests will also have a pleasant time. Your own freedom will make your guests feel relaxed, comfortable and welcome in your home.

Don't Compromise

When hosting unbelievers, do not compromise your Christian witness by allowing activities or conversation that would be contrary to your personal standards. The way that you behave in your home can be the best example to others of your convictions.

Maintain an Edifying Atmosphere

Questionable music, ungodly television and gossip are all poor ingredients for an evening of edifying fellowship. The atmosphere is up to you.

What Should I Do for Different Types of Entertaining?

There are many different people groups that will cross your path, and you will have to do many different types of entertaining. Again, I would like to suggest a few tips for some of these varying events in your home. I am sure that you will have many more experiences in hospitality than I could list here. However, perhaps some of these tips will stimulate some additional ideas.

Please do not take any of these recommendations as legalistic religious duties. They are merely intended as suggestions to spark your own creative ideas that fit you, your family and your friends.

Family–On a Daily Basis

Make it a habit to set the table nicely. Your family members are the truest riches in your home and deserve the warmest hospitality.

Serve them the best food frequently. In other words, do not always save the best for guests. This is not to say that guests should not receive the best that the family budget can afford. However, if the family only receives the best cut of the day when guests arrive at the door, they will not feel that they really are the most valuable to you.

Be creative, and make your home an enjoyable place. Keeping your home in order and prepared to receive guests is important, but not more important than allowing a child to play with toys in the house, or a young baker to experiment with the mysteries of the kitchen.

Keep your home open and prepared for your children's friends. Make it a warm and inviting place for them to be as well. You will experience the joy of having your children around more often if their friends feel welcome in your home and at your table. It is truly amazing that God multiplies the grocery budget when your heart is open to the "children of the harvest."

Special Family Times–Birthdays, Anniversaries, Holidays, Etc.

One of the basic goals for the family should be to build happy memories for its members. Each family likes and needs its own unique traditions. These traditions need not be expensive; they should simply be unique to the family. Celebrating special family times is not only appropriate, but gives the individual family members a feeling of belonging and identification–a sense of roots.

Casual Entertaining

Keep it simple. Be sensitive to your guests' needs. Do not shy away from good, spiritual conversation or simple table games.

Showing a video may be appropriate for a portion of the evening if it helps stimulate good conversation before and after it's shown. However, showing a video that is unedifying or has not been previewed beforehand is pointless, at best, and dangerous to your reputation as a hostess. Remember, the goal is not just entertaining–the goal is hospitality. Sadly, these two are sometimes worlds apart.

Sit Down Dinner Parties

Plan ahead. Invitations should be made two to three weeks or more in advance or sooner, depending on the season. Be aware of how many places your table seats comfortably. Be aware of the diet habits of your guests. Be sensitive to your guests, and be pleasantly aware of their children's needs. Plan ahead for children. When you touch the life of a child in a special way, you touch the parents also!

Allow the meal to be an expression of yourself. Do not attempt to create a meal that is beyond your culinary skills or your budget! Your guests will love you for being you. Do not practice untested recipes on your guests. When serving appetizers, plan only one or two hot appetizers that will need to be heated at the last minute. The other appetizers should be cold, requiring little or no last minute attention. Serve appetizers or special drinks in the living room.

Prior to serving dinner, simply state what you will be serving to drink, and ask for preferences. Also, ask if your guests would prefer their drinks with dinner or after dinner. Have all food on the table and ready to serve before directing your guests to the table, unless you are serving the meal course by course. Food should pass to the left, unless someone has already started it to the right. Usually, guests will look to the host or hostess to begin the direction for passing the food.

Buffet Style Dinner Parties

Know how many people you can serve comfortably in your home. Be sure that each guest has a place to sit and a place to rest a glass or plate. Have that place obviously prepared with coasters for the drinks, if needed. Dinnerware and napkins should usually be set out on the buffet table, but they may also be needed in the area where the guests are sitting.

If your home is small, the food does not have to be all in one place. The hot food may be near the stove or oven, the salad and relish dishes in the dining area and the dinnerware and glasses on a small table. Just be sure that traffic flows easily. Do a practice walk-through to test it out before your guests arrive.

Potluck Dinner Parties

Prepare a general theme or menu well in advance. Notify people of what they should bring at least two weeks ahead of time. This helps them to adjust their grocery budgets appropriately. Usually, it is appropriate to ask each family to bring two items (for example, a main dish and a dessert) that feed six to eight people. Each single person should be asked to bring one item that will feed six to eight people.

Do not insult single adults by asking them to bring only the simple items, such as butter and rolls or ice cream. Cooking is not an art for married people only. There are probably as many single adults who enjoy cooking and have delicious recipes to offer as there are married people who do. Some singles may prefer bringing the simple items, but some may not. Never assume—always ask.

Never overlook the senior citizens at these gatherings either. Generally, they like to bring food and want to be acknowledged that they too are a needed part of the Body. They probably have some of the most tested and tasty recipes in the entire group. However, you must be extremely aware of their limited budgets or their varying abilities to get to a grocery store. To sense their individual desires and abilities in this area, talk to them at a point in time when there are no upcoming commitments.

Arranging food at a long table, buffet style is generally acceptable. Place food and utensils in a practical order that will allow a smooth flow of traffic. The plates should be first, and the drinks and desserts should be last. However, do not limit your creativity. Setting up family style and passing food from table to table can be fun too.

Small Groups–Home Meetings or Bible Study Groups

Be well prepared before guests arrive. The bathroom should have appropriate supplies within view (such as extra toilet paper, disinfectant spray, soap and a hand towel).

A table should be prepared for refreshments prior to the meeting. If someone else is bringing them, ask if he or she could possibly arrive a few minutes early. Refreshments should be simple but delicious and attractively arranged.

A bedroom, guestroom or office should be prepared with a chair or two for mothers who need to feed their babies or for those needing personal prayer or counseling. Communicate with young mothers concerning this available place upon their arrival, so as not to cause them to feel awkward during the meeting.

Appropriate seating should be arranged in a logical order. Be sure that the primary host or speaker is easily within view of most guests.

Prepare a place for coats and hats. Work as a team with your spouse or another person. One should answer the door and take coats while the other sees that everyone is finding appropriate seating. You may want to serve coffee, tea, or a cold drink at this time also.

Be at peace with everyone in your home prior to the arrival of the guests. The mood of your relationships may be reflected in the atmosphere of the meeting. The television should be turned off and newspapers and magazines put away fifteen to thirty minutes prior to the scheduled arrival time. Turning on edifying music at this time will help prepare your family for the ministry that is set before them, as well as initially aiding the introductory atmosphere for the guests.

If there are candles around the home, light them five minutes before you expect the first person to arrive, or as your hospitality team member answers the first knock. This will be dependent, of course, upon how many candles have to be lit! Candles can add a relaxing touch to the atmosphere. However, candles should not be within the reach of small children.

Bridal or Baby Showers

Be sure that the honored guest will enjoy what you have planned. Communicate with her about her desires well in advance, and be prepared ahead of time. Your preparation may increase the security level or the anxiety level of your honored guest concerning her shower.

Invite her friends and family members, and be sensitive to any unsaved guests who may be coming. Usually, formal invitations in some form are necessary for a successful shower, whether by phone or by mail.

Plan a couple of short games or a testimony time that most people will enjoy. Asking everyone present to introduce themselves and explain how they know or are related to the honored guest is often a nice means of warming up the atmosphere and sparking conversation among guests. If you have someone share, be sure to limit the sharing to approximately ten to fifteen minutes. This is not an appropriate time for teaching, unless the honored guest has specifically requested it. This will need to be communicated with the person who is sharing prior to the shower, so as not to cause offense when you ask them to speak.

Some couples prefer that these celebrations include the bride and the groom, or both the mother and the father of the newborn. Whatever they prefer is appropriate. There are no set rules. It's their party–do what they prefer, not what you prefer.

Overnight Guests

Make yourself aware of your guest's diet habits by simply asking.

If the guest is using another family member's room, remove all items that will be needed before the guest arrives. If the guest is sharing a bathroom with others in the family, lay clean, nicely folded towels on his or her bed or dresser.

Be sure that there is clean bedding on the bed. Lay an extra blanket across the foot of the bed, or mention to the guest where one can be easily located if he or she needs it. Closet space and empty hangers should be available in the room where the guest is sleeping. A clock and clean mirror should be in the room. If the room is large enough, it is nice to provide a chair.

A welcome basket on the bed or dresser is warm and inviting. This basket could include items, such as pen and paper, a clean glass for the bathroom, fruit, mints, small toilet articles, a small article that represents something significant about your city or region, a "we're so glad you're here" note, etc. Be creative. Keep this basket simple. Let it be another reflection of Jesus in you!

Overnight Guest Ministers

As with any overnight guest, make yourself aware of his or her diet habits simply by asking. If you have young children, let them be themselves, but be sure that they are being respectful of your guest's need for privacy. Do not let them crawl on the guest. Also, be sure that the children are being sensitive to the guest's need to use the bathroom, if the bathroom is being shared with other family members.

Be aware of the guest's need for rest. Do not keep him or her up late, sharing, praying or counseling with you. If this type of personal ministry is needed, make it part of the arranged ministry schedule.

If you and your husband are responsible for arranging the guest's ministry schedule, be sure that the guest has a simple, typewritten itinerary of planned events. You may want to schedule specific meeting times, a guided tour of the church building and meeting rooms, rest times, shopping times, dining times, etc.

Be aware of the guest's need to pray, study or meditate on the Word. Provide a quiet, appropriate atmosphere. Usually, ministers need some time to get focused before they minister. They do not need incessant conversation to feel welcome in your home.

If the guest has been extensively traveling just prior to his or her arrival, offer to do laundry for them. If the guest prefers to do it themselves, offer to show him or her how to use your laundry facilities.

If the guest has small children along, offer a night light for the bedroom, and be sure to have one in the bathroom. If your guest is sharing the bathroom with other family members, communicate scheduled times that he or she may feel free to shower. Asking the guest's preference is best. Be sure to show the guest where you keep fresh towels and where you prefer for him or her to put soiled towels. In the bathroom, be sure to clean the mirror, shine the chrome, clean and shine the tub, and provide fresh soap, room deodorizer, a night light, a lock on the door, and extra toilet tissue in obvious places. If the bathroom is too small to make the extra toilet tissue obvious, then be sure to tell your guest where it's stored.

As with other overnight guests, a welcome basket on the bed or dresser is warm and inviting. A small bouquet of flowers may also be appropriate.

How Does My Hospitality Demonstrate Christ in Me?

Although this chapter has read like an endless list of practical suggestions, surely the outworking of Christianity through the avenue of hospitality is one of the most practical ways that we can be "doers of the Word and not hearers only," as James says. Again, please read these suggestions as possibilities to consider.

So many opportunities, and so little time! Opportunities for hospitality are certainly all around us. Every person who you meet will have a need at some point in time for the spirit of hospitality to flow from you. You do not need to be eloquent of speech, have an elaborate home or be an exquisite chef; you simply need to be willing to open your heart through a practical demonstration of the nature of Christ. Hospitality can be expressed through wholesome conversation, popcorn or fresh towels. It's not complicated really; it's just essential to true Christian compassion.

May you be ever mindful to "make His joy complete" by not looking "only to your own interests, but also to the interests of others" (Philippians 2:2-4).

Chapter 8

GRACE

A Woman of Distinction

✣

Another aspect of walking in your calling and anointing is being a woman of grace in the public eye. The magnitude of this responsibility can quickly send you back to the joy of folding towels in the privacy of your own home. Whether going public means having a heart-searching conversation with your local pharmacist or addressing a thousand people, you can still sense the importance of your mission and feel the need to rely upon Christ's grace and anointing.

Some people have a unique grace to speak with people one-on-one. When they do, it usually results in a meaningful and edifying interchange. Others have a unique grace to speak to groups of people. When they do, it often results in individual and corporate edification. Each person's gift ministers to the individual or stirs vision in the group as a whole. Each person also usually stands in wonder of the other's gift. Often, what neither realizes is that the other, though gifted in one area, is often insecure in the other. You may be proficient in both of these areas, but you probably have to focus on developing one of them more than the other.

I can remember the first time my husband and I were guest speakers for a specific out of town singles' group. A young man, whom we did not know, was sent to the airport to pick us up. We were a bit tired from our long flight, adjusting to the change in climate, and we had a long drive ahead of us to the retreat center. We did our best, we thought, to be friendly to our young host. He asked us a few questions, and we did the same in return. When we seemed to have run out of dialogue, there were long periods of silence and an occasional observant comment on the scenery as we continued down the road. We felt very comfortable and welcomed by our warm host.

After the weekend of teaching, praying, and recreating with the group, our young driver approached us with gratitude in his eyes. He had felt challenged and ministered to throughout the weekend. He was now making a genuine effort to compliment us by saying, "When I picked you up at the airport and drove you here, I thought you weren't going to have much to say. Boy, was I surprised! I really was ministered to this weekend."

Both of us looked at each other, thanked the young man for both the drive and the compliment, and went to our room to pack, feeling just a little insecure. Obviously, the periods of silence during the drive to the retreat center had sent an inaccurate message. We realized at that point that even though we could speak to a group, every public encounter with people is important, and we needed to work on our one-on-one encounters.

Each of us feels a different measure of grace for ministering to people in different settings. Whether the setting is in the context of a large group, a small group, or with an individual, we all have different comfort zones in our ability to relate to people in a public sense.

What if your personal identification card indicated that you were a Christian? What if every time you purchased something at a store or restaurant you had to show an identification card that exposed your Christianity to the person you were facing? What if in that moment the individual you encountered made his or her decision for Christ based on your conversation or behavior? Would that change anything about your behavior?

II Corinthians 3:3 says, "Clearly you are an epistle of Christ, ministered by us, written not with ink but by the Spirit of the living

God, not on tablets of stone but on tablets of flesh, that is, of the heart." We all go public nearly every day. Whether with one person or many, we are all being read. Whether we like it or not, some people will make their decisions for Christ based on what they read in us.

How Should I Respond to Public Expectations?

There are certain vocations that carry with them a greater responsibility to be in the public eye. People in these vocations are expected to respond publicly in an appropriate manner whenever they are called upon to do so. Christians in these vocations have very high expectations placed on them.

These vocations vary, from political representative to sports hero, from real estate agent to dentist. Whether you have a professional career, lead a ministry in the church, or volunteer as a tutor or coach for the local high school, there will be times when you may find yourself in the eye of the public. Secular and spiritual environments both need more Christ-centered women, who are willing to be at the forefront, leading with grace in their demeanor and the law of kindness in their speech.

Whether you are outgoing or shy by nature, people will expect you to be conversational when they are reticent and reserved when they are sanguine, simply because you are a Christian. Your personality type or individual trials will not matter to them at the time of contact. They will simply expect you to be what they think a Christian should be. There really is not much that you can do to adjust the expectations of others. I sometimes wonder if God allows this inclination just to keep us dependent upon His grace.

I have known a number of pastors and Christian men in professional positions who have told others that expectations should not be put on their wives simply because of their own positions. This tactic may work temporarily, but it won't last forever, especially not if you're planning on your business or church growing. As new people come into the church or company, they too will have their predisposed definitions of how Christian leaders and their wives should function.

As a wife, even if you have done your best to dismiss yourself from any role of leadership, people will still look to you for some evidence of care at given opportunities. If you remove yourself from all responsibilities and are focused on another career, your lack of involvement or show of concern will still communicate a message. Whether you like it or not, even if you have your own separate career, people do place expectations on the wives of church or corporate leaders. There is no way to avoid this; you must be willing to be in the public eye and cannot hide behind someone else's title to get out of it.

Accept the fact that certain things will be expected of you that will not be expected of others, simply because you are a Christian. Co-workers, peers, and family members will expect you to model Christian virtue and feminine boldness simultaneously. They will expect you to do this for the sake of all younger women, who need a role model of successful womanhood.

The expectations of others may not be fair, but they are reality. The harder you fight against these expectations, the less you will enjoy what God has in store for you in the midst of it all. There is nothing that He has called you to that He will not give you the grace to fulfill.

I would like to address three areas of public interaction in which all Christians may find themselves involved: making the first impression, having proper platform persona and being involved at the forefront with appropriate greetings and introductions.

How Can I Make a Good Impression?

First impressions last a long time in the minds of most people. Making a good first impression can actually be wrapped up in three simple steps: be approachable, learn names and faces and respond conversationally.

Be Approachable

Approachability is significant in Christendom. Some would go so far as to say that it is an earmark of Christianity.

Smile

The number one key to this is simply to smile. Smiling is an outward demonstration of your approachability, your care and concern for others. It communicates warmth and openness. It helps people to feel that they can trust you.

Smiling while you are speaking with people on the telephone puts warmth in the tone of your voice when your countenance cannot be seen. This may sound silly, but it does work. Test it out between family members, and see if they can tell when you are smiling.

Now you may not feel comfortable walking around with a full-fledged smile on your face all the time. In fact, you may feel that people who do are a little suspicious. However, working at having a warm, open countenance is essential.

Be aware of those times when you are concentrating heavily on something. Sometimes, when you're thinking of something other than your present circumstance, your face can carry a look of consternation instead of openness. For example, walk through the grocery store sometime and look at the face of another shopper, who is staring at their groceries while they are being added up. What do you see? Is it a look of approachability? Probably not–this shopper's mind is probably else-where. He or she does not intend to look disgruntled or uncaring, but probably does.

Think about how you look when you're letting your thoughts wan-der. You may never get a chance to speak to someone if your counte-nance scares him or her from a distance.

Greet People

Greeting people verbally and physically, with a handshake or appropriate touch, communicates approachability as well.

This varies from culture to culture, of course. In some Asian cultures, only a bow or a handshake would be appropriate. In some Latin cultures, a light kiss to each cheek is polite and appropriate. Once, two of our church missionary families returned home on the same weekend to have weddings for their adult children. Seeing their teenage children after a service, I proceeded to greet them. Much to my dismay, I hugged those from the Asian culture and bowed to those from the Latin culture! My circuits got crossed! Fortunately, among Christian brothers and sisters in Christ, these kinds of situations can usually be remedied with a second chance.

In the United States, greeting styles vary from region to region and church to church. Sometimes they even vary from person to person. People, who have grown up in a very loving, affectionate family environment, tend to be more physical in their greetings. However, people, who have grown up in homes or families where there has not been much outward display of affection, tend not to be so easily open or trusting of an immediate display of affection. We each have our own personal comfort zones that we allow others to enter. Always be sensitive to these zones. It is usually better to err on the conservative side, rather than on the more liberal side of this issue.

Greet People in Passing

Another gesture that communicates approachability is greeting people when you are passing them, whether in the hallway at church, on the street corner, or at the nearby market. People love attention. Generally speaking, they love it when you initiate contact with them. This is true for people of all ages, from the youngest to the oldest.

Be careful not to treat youth or older people as though they are invisible. A young person may be too intimidated to speak to you first. An older person may not be able to keep up with your stride as you hurriedly rush from place to place. Remember, as a Christian, people are your business. You are here to serve and to minister to people. Your motivation should always be to serve the individual, as well as the corporate group, not the other way around.

Several years ago, someone came to observe our church and its leadership team. Toward the end of his weeklong stay with us, my husband asked him about some of his observations. He humorously said that we were like "ants on speed!" ("Speed" meaning the methamphetamine drug.) He had many kind and gracious things to say also. However, this observation is the one that has remained in our minds to this day.

In the midst of your busyness to get substantial business for the Lord done, whether inside church walls or out, work hard at appearing not to be consumed with busyness. People will not seek out those who always look busy. Generally speaking, the average person will not stop someone who looks like he or she does not want to be deterred from arriving at his or her destination as soon as possible. The bold person may, but the most needy one probably will not.

While Jesus walked on this earth, He constantly surprised the disciples by stopping to speak to individuals who seemed to be blocking the way. Do not get so hurried that you overlook people. As you go from one place to the next or from one meeting to the next, allow yourself time to be interrupted on the way. Slow your pace, put a smile on your face, and actually greet the people who you might normally pass by. You may run into an "angel" that you would have otherwise overlooked in your quick pace.

Look People in the Eye

One further comment on this area of approachability is to be sure that you look people in the eye when you are speaking to them. Eye contact is essential in good communication. Don't look over a person's shoulder or down at the floor as you speak to him or her. Look the person in the eye. This validates his or her worth to you. If you constantly look away from someone's countenance, it can cause him or her to feel that you're uncomfortable for some reason. It also may communicate that you would prefer to be speaking with another person, rather than to him or her.

There is, of course, inappropriate eye contact. When you are communicating, do not look at a person from the top of the head to the bottom of the feet, or stop at any other part of his or her anatomy along the way. This may make the person feel that you are sizing up his or her worth based on physical appearance. It may also communicate inappropriate intentions. Do not stare at the person constantly while he or she is speaking. Eye contact is essential, but constant eye contact for a long period of time needs to be broken occasionally. It is helpful to have something in your hand to nonchalantly glance at to break the stare. However, looking at your watch would be inappropriate. If a person is in the middle of a rather long comment, it is important to look away occasionally.

Maintain Good Hygiene

A final aspect of approachability is making sure that your hygiene and grooming habits are such that people are not offended or put off by a lack of cleanliness. Diligently take care of yourself; literally be clean and smell fresh. Bad body odor and halitosis can be a genuine hindrance to your approachability and your effectiveness as a witness for Christ.

Have you ever prayed for someone that you wanted to give a breath mint to before you even began? Hopefully, you were able to focus your compassion and pray effectively despite your personal offense. Or have you ever gone to the altar specifically to pray for people and noticed that several other altar workers standing down the row from you had three people waiting in line for prayer and you had none? Maybe you needed to check your breath and your armpits!

Have you ever sat on a public bus near someone with bad body odor and felt waves of nausea overcoming you? Were you motivated to share Christ, or head for the nearest exit? Or have you ever sat on the bus and noticed people moving away from you, even though you showered just an hour prior to this? Maybe you needed to check if it was time for your coat to go to the dry cleaner. Your influence at that moment may not have gone the direction you wanted it to.

Additionally, I Corinthians 11: 15 tells us that a woman's hair is her glory. Your hair should always be clean and looking its best. Do your best to have it styled in such a way that it frames your face nicely and brings the onlooker's eye immediately to your countenance.

Good hygiene is essential to being approachable. Being a woman of grace not only means maintaining good hygiene, but also means being approachable despite the hygiene of another.

Learn Names And Faces

Another aspect of making a good first impression is to learn names and faces. The primary key is to be sure that you hear the person's name precisely the first time. If you are unsure that you've heard it correctly, ask him or her to repeat it or even spell it for you. With people from other nations, it may even be necessary to write out the name phonetically for your own remembrance. People love it when others know their names, and they are even more impressed when their names are pronounced correctly at the second encounter. To do so, you have to get their names correct the first time.

Repeating the name once or twice in the conversation helps to lodge it in your own thoughts. Writing the name down, perhaps with a brief description of the individual, will also help you to remember. Noticing a unique or striking feature, like the color of the person's eyes, hairstyle or a unique facial feature, may help. The more of your five senses that you use in moments like these, the more the name will become engraved in your mind.

Learning names and faces is just one more way of validating a person's value. For some, this may motivate their first step toward salvation as they see Christ in you through this avenue of care and concern. For others, who are believers already, it may simply be the needed boost for their daily walks, or it may initiate the healing of wounded spirits. The small things like these count for so very much!

Respond Conversationally

The third aspect that communicates approachability is responding conversationally. Basically, conversational responses come in two forms: verbal signs and non-verbal signs.

Non-Verbal Signs

Non-verbal signs are simply signs that communicate to the other person that you are listening. These signs demonstrate your interest. (Again, some of these may vary from culture to culture.)

Listening actively, not passively, is key. No physical gesture you make to demonstrate that you are listening can supersede actual, active listening. Just as you can tell when someone is really listening to you, other people can too. You may get by with distracted listening sometimes, but it will not serve you well in the long run. Be focused on the conversation that you are presently involved in. Otherwise, you may find yourself being counted a fool. Paraphrased, Proverbs 18:13 says, "A fool answers before he hears."

As with introductions, maintaining eye contact is essential in responding conversationally. Nodding your head in agreement or disagreement and changing your facial expressions as the other person speaks are all clues of active listening.

If the conversation is one that will warrant further thought or future decision making, taking down a few notes will demonstrate your interest in the other person's perspective on the matter.

Verbal Signs

Verbal signs, as with non-verbal signs, vary from culture to culture and region to region. Verbal responses also indicate that you value what the other person is saying.

Your first verbal response should be to demonstrate that you understand what the other person said. Saying "Yes" or "No" or " That's right" shows that you understand and are staying with the speaker in the conversation.

Responding to what the other person is saying, before interjecting your own perspective or before the subject is changed, is also important. Use simple statements, such as "Yes, I understand," "I see. That's a really good point," "That's interesting. I'm really glad you told me that." Any of these statements could be possible responses, as long as they relate appropriately to the previous statement.

Expressing genuine concern and an accurate awareness of someone's concerns without making a statement that will project the conversation into a negative and faithless direction is important also. Make a simple response, like "That must be frustrating at times," or "I'm so sorry. How could I best help you with that?"

Again, making a good first impression is key to being in the eye of the public and being an effective witness for Christ. Approachability, learning names and faces, and responding conversationally are all-important ingredients that will aid in doing this effectively.

What Is Proper Platform Persona?

Whether you are a pastor, a church staff member or a member of the congregation, you may find yourself on the church platform from time to time. You may be called upon to lead in prayer, make an announcement, sing a special song or a variety of other things. When you least expect it, you may find yourself at the forefront of the congregation.

This, as with so many other things that I have mentioned in this chapter, varies from culture to culture, region to region, church to church. What may be in vogue in one congregation could be offensive in another congregation. What one leader may feel is exemplary to create the atmosphere of a congregation may be the opposite of what someone else may feel.

Fashion and Modesty

Some women in leadership feel that the best quality dress, high-heeled shoes, hair extensions and artistically designed fingernails are the examples they want to set before the congregation. This may be to help motivate the women in the congregation to be their very best in the house of God and to exemplify that God graciously meets our needs abundantly.

Others may be put off by such attire and may want to wear shorts and tank tops, have simple hairstyles and go without nail polish or shoes, for that matter. This may be motivated by the desire to create an atmosphere in which people can come to relax, be refreshed in God's presence, without the worry of impressing anyone by their outward appearance.

Then, some will put off by both of these approaches and will want to be somewhere in between. This approach may be motivated by the desire to be able to relate to both of the groups aforementioned and everyone in between.

Regardless of the style of dress that you choose to wear, let it be a reflection of you, and let it be an example, a model to others. Whether you consider yourself an example or not, you are if you are at the forefront. Do not try to be someone other then yourself, and don't project an image that doesn't fit your personality. Instead, try to reflect the nature of Christ, not only in what you say and do, but also in how you present yourself outwardly.

As the Bible says in I Samuel 16:7, ". . . for man looks at the outward appearance, but the Lord looks at the heart." We like to emphasize the part that says, ". . . the Lord looks at the heart," to relieve any feelings of restraint. However, the verse does say, ". . . man looks at the outward appearance." Because of this, you may have to adjust some of what you wear, not because of how it looks on you, but because of the example it may set for young people or new converts. What may be fine on you may not be fine on others.

Inappropriate dress can also be a hindrance to effectiveness. If people are struggling with or distracted by what you are wearing because it is immodest, they will also struggle with being able to hear your message. Some blouses may be appropriate to wear while standing up, but not while kneeling over someone in prayer at the altar. Some skirt lengths may be appropriate for standing, but not for bending over or sitting on a chair that is two feet above the front row of the group that you are addressing. As tedious as it is, all of these placements and postures should be considered when you plan to be ministering on the platform or at the altar.

When you received your calling, you may not have been aware of it, but you gave God permission to get into your closet. Surprisingly, He gave a few other people permission to influence your wardrobe as well. This can seem unfair and be frustrating at times. However, if Jesus was willing to die for the sake of the gospel, a wardrobe adjustment on our parts should not be beyond our sacrificial service, for the sake of sharing the gospel with someone who may be easily offended.

The main principal by which we should abide is found in I Timothy 2:9-10, ". . . that the women adorn themselves in modest apparel, with propriety and moderation . . ." This principle applies whether you are on the platform, in the congregation or in your workplace.

Granted, modesty has different definitions in different cultures. In some cultures showing your midriff may be appropriate, while in others, it may be considered suggestive. In some cultures, wearing pants is appropriate, while in others, pants are considered male attire only. In some cultures, nail polish is considered beautiful, while in others, it is considered worldly. Learn what is acceptable in your own culture, and do your best to represent Christian modesty.

The main issue is not your liberty, but modeling and sharing Christ where He has placed you. If He has indeed placed you there, He will give you the grace to enjoy yourself in the situation if you will yield yourself to Him. His grace definitely brings definition and balance to what we sacrifice for Him and what we sacrifice for others. Change is not always necessary; however, the willingness to change usually is.

Immodest dress can send mixed signals. It can be very confusing and can cause you to be a poor example of a godly believer. Mature people may pity your naivete or simply not take your testimony seriously. Young followers, on the other hand, may be confused and hindered in their spiritual growth as they attempt to follow your example. If your external beauty conflicts with your internal beauty, the purposes God has for those following you may be thwarted.

We each need to honestly recognize our differing body-types and dress ourselves accordingly. The more sexually desirable attributes that a woman has, the harder she has to work to cover herself modestly.

If you have a large bust, do not dress like you don't. You simply cannot wear certain types of tops that others can wear, and be modest too. If you do dress this way, men may struggle in their ability to clearly hear the gospel message that you are presenting. Your outward appearance may distract their attention from your inward person, as well as from your message.

We each have to accept the way the Lord made us, keep our sense of humor in tact, and enjoy the benefits of our own special blessings. Wisdom and modesty are the great equalizers when it comes to the presentation of body-types. Always allow Jesus to guide you in this very important area.

Of course, the simple response to all of this would be to always purchase clothes that are appropriate no matter what situation you may find yourself in. Obviously, this is not always going to be possible. However, be especially aware of hemlines and necklines, especially when you know that you may be called upon for active duty in a public setting.

Active Participation in the Church Service

What is more important than what you are wearing while you are on the church platform is that you are an active participant in the service. This is crucial to your platform ministry. In other words, worship during the worship portion of the service; do not be looking for that person you need to see after the service. Actively listen and respond to whoever is at the podium speaking, regardless of what part of the service he or she is addressing. Is the sermon more important than holy communion? Is communion more important than the exhortation to give tithes and offerings? Is giving tithes and offerings more important than the announcements, nursery children or choir? No, one is not more important than the other, and we should not dismiss the importance of different parts of the service by our own lack of attentiveness.

People constantly watch whoever is sitting on the platform, and they will model your attentiveness or lack of it. You would probably be amazed to know how the teens and young adults of your congregation will model your public performance on their own time. Much to your own embarrassment, your behavior may even show up in a skit when you least expect it.

Some pastors attempt to eliminate this distraction by not having anyone on the platform except the person who is leading a specific part of the service. They choose to have the rest of the ministry team sit on the front row instead. This may eliminate some of the distraction, but people will still pay attention to the example of those before them. Whether you sit on the platform or in the front row, you cannot avoid the fact that people will watch you if you are one of the church leaders or assisting in a service. God created us as sheep that look to a shepherd to follow.

Obviously, you will not always be perfect in your example, but do your best to be as active a participant on the platform (or front row) as you would want others in the congregation to be. Be the best that you can be for the Lord, and you will be the best that you can be for those who are following your example.

What Should I Do When I am at the Forefront?

You may feel called to be a leader in the church congregation or a leader on the job. If you do, here are just a few practical tips that will help when you are speaking to a group. You may not feel called to do any public speaking whatsoever, but rather feel to lead in a variety of ways through administration, music or helps. Whether you feel called to be a public speaker or not, you probably will be called upon, at some time, to give a motivational greeting or introduction to a small group, large corporate gathering or church congregation. Hence, I would like to share the basics of how to give an appropriate greeting and introduction.

You should be able to stand up and say more than, "Hi. I'd rather be here than in any hospital in the city." You also should be able to introduce someone with more than, "Well, here is our speaker." What you have to say at these times should be inspirational, but succinct.

Greeting a Corporate Group

First, let's determine how to give an appropriate greeting. The purpose of a greeting should always be to edify the Body of Christ, to encourage and inspire the listeners in a brief amount of time.

Dressing appropriately and smiling are, of course, vital to releasing your own confidence. By "appropriate," I mean whatever is appropriate for the occasion, whether a dress or jeans. If you are not dressed appropriately, smile as though you are. Draw the group's attention to your countenance and away from what you have on by your smile and confidence.

Once, I was traveling from the West Coast to speak at a ladies' retreat in upstate New York. I had two flights on major airlines, and my last flight was on a very small airplane that required me to wear large headphones to handle the cabin pressure. All three of my flights were wonderfully smooth, even the one in the very small plane, which was flown by one of the church members. However, due to the use of the large headphones, by the time that I arrived at my destination, my hair-do was "undone," to say the least.

The pilot was to drive me to the pastor's home, but told me that there was a mid-week service going on at the church and asked if I would like to drop in for a minute just to see the relatively new church building. Although I was not dressed for church, I agreed.

We slipped into the back of the service and took our seats. My pilot disappeared, and the next thing I realized, the pastor was saying, "Oh, I see that Glenda has arrived for the ladies' retreat. Why don't you come up and greet the church." Well, I could think of a few reasons right away as to why I should not come up and greet the church. I was tired and feeling really unspiritual, I was not appropriately dressed for the service, and, most of all, my "do" was "undone!" However, I smiled, walked to the front, as though I was dressed for Easter Sunday service, and greeted the church. So, first and foremost, smile and walk confidently to the podium.

If you feel over-anxious or nervous for any reason, because of the way you look or because you do not know what to say, walk confidently and trust the Lord to put His Words in your mouth. Your job is not to get the nervous "butterflies" in your stomach to disappear, but just to make them "fly in formation." Nervousness can work for you if you let it push you to dependence on the Lord in moments like these.

For those moments when you feel the least inspirational, it is wise to have at least one thing in your speaking repertoire that you can share in just a few minutes.

A simple greeting should be just that–simple. It usually should be no longer than five minutes, unless the person in charge requests otherwise. If the person leading the meeting has instructed you to take fifteen or twenty minutes, it is wise to briefly mention that to the group. Simply say, "I have been asked to take about fifteen minutes to share with you." This is needed because some people may begin to feel resentful that you are taking time from the main speaker if they do not realize that you have been requested to speak for so long. Mentioning this sets them at ease and motivates them to listen to what you have to say.

Paul begins all of his epistles with a greeting to the people. If you are unsure of how to do this, just follow his example. Not all of these will work for a non-Christian gathering; however, similar principles would apply. Allow me to suggest a few tips from Paul's pattern.

Pronounce a Blessing

Pronounce a blessing on the people. This actually could be first or last in your greeting. Simply say something like, "God bless you!" In Romans 1:7, Paul said, ". . . Grace to you and peace from God our Father and the Lord Jesus Christ." In I Corinthians 1:3 he says virtually the same thing. This shows that this part of Paul's greeting was second nature to him; it flowed out of his spirit easily and freely. Obviously, if you are greeting a non-Christian organization, you may not want to start with this. Slipping it in at the end may be more appropriate.

Express Thankfulness for the Opportunity

Express thankfulness for the opportunity to be with them. In Romans 1:8, Paul says, "First, I thank my God through Jesus Christ for you all, that your faith is spoken of throughout the whole world."

Express Appreciation for the Leadership

Express appreciation and respect for those leading the service, seminar or meeting. In Colossians 4:7, Paul gives a final greeting, beginning with, "Tychicus, a beloved brother, faithful minister, and fellow servant in the Lord . . ."

Express Thankfulness for Your Audience

Express thankfulness for your audience, and commend them in some way. In I Thessalonians 1:2-3, Paul says, "We give thanks to God always for you all, making mention of you in our prayers, remembering without ceasing your work of faith, labor of love, and patience of hope in our Lord Jesus Christ in the sight of our God and Father . . ." If you are speaking in a church service, you might want to mention something meaningful about the worship service, the choir or a special song that was sung. If you are speaking at a business meeting, you might commend the administrative team, the organization of the meeting schedule or a variety of other things.

Express Your Personal Love for the Lord

In Ephesians 1:3, Paul says, "Blessed be the God and Father of our Lord Jesus Christ, who has blessed us with every spiritual blessing in the heavenly places in Christ . . ." Mention something of His good works in your life or something with which He is currently challenging you.

Make a Special Request for Prayer

This is a possibility, depending on the situation. In II Thessalonians 3:1-2, Paul writes, "Finally, brethren, pray for us, that the word of the Lord may run swiftly and be glorified, just as it is with you, and that we may be delivered from unreasonable and wicked men; for not all have faith." Other requests might be for specific financial projects or the needs of groups or individuals that the group is supporting.

Add a Short Exhortation

Add a short five to ten minute exhortation to your greeting when the leader has requested that you do so. For this to be effective, you must be sure that it is not only concise, but that it also has clear points. Otherwise, it may be momentarily inspirational, but it will not be remembered. I Corinthians 1:6-9 and Philippians 1:5-6 are good illustrations of brief and effective exhortations.

Introducing a Speaker

Now, let's consider the issue of introducing a speaker. The purpose for an introduction is to build rapport between the speaker and the listeners. If you set the stage by being awkward and nervous, the main speaker will have to spend time getting the audience in a relaxed and receptive frame of mind. That should be your job.

An introduction should be brief, positive and interesting. It should be approximately two to three minutes and absolutely no longer than five minutes. Again, if you take longer than this, the congregation may become resentful that you are taking the speaker's time.

As with greetings, you should be dressed appropriately for the occasion, smile and do your best to look confident.

If the room is a bit too cool, do not wear a coat on the platform. You want to give the appearance that you have confidence it will warm up soon. You want the focus to be on what the speaker has to say, not on the temperature of the room. If the room is frigid however, you may wear your coat to the podium, make a positive humorous comment and, again, bring the focus back to the speaker. If the room is too warm, ignore it while you are at the podium. After your introduction, see to it that the room will either be cooled down or have some kind of air circulation flowing through it while the speaker is speaking. Do your best to see that the room is neither too warm nor too cold. However, cool is better than warm, as some members of the audience may fall asleep if it is too warm.

Prior to introducing someone to a group, I recommend that you do a brief interview with that person. In your interview answer the questions "Who," "Where," "What" and "Why." Even if you feel that you know the person really well, you may want to ask him or her questions relating to the topic he or she will be speaking on. Your job, again, is to build rapport between the speaker and the audience, and part of that may be to connect the message with the hearts of the listeners. Do an interview, and then give part of what you learned in the interview with the actual introduction. Always find out more than you actually need to know.

Now, here are a few suggestions for the introduction.

Who?

Be sure to pronounce the speaker's name correctly. It is far better to embarrass yourself before the meeting by repeating it back and asking if you're saying it correctly, than to have the speaker correct you in front of the group. Some speakers will let a mispronounced name slide by with no correction, but some will not. Everyone likes people to know how to pronounce their name correctly. As you're introducing the speaker and pronouncing his or her name correctly, also say how glad you are that he or she is able to be with the group today.

Where?

Mention where the speaker is from. This might include the nation, state, city, church or business group.

What?

Give the speaker's credentials, both spiritual and natural. Be careful to not give too much detail; make it interesting, but not overstated. Overstating a person's credentials is usually obvious and weakens the impression of the listener more than strengthening it. Your goal is to stir the listener's desire to hear the speaker. Some of the "what" may include the speaker's marital status, number of children, educational background, occupation or a special portion of his or her personal testimony that either relates to the topic or uniquely relates to the listeners. Again, do not give all of this information, only give some of it.

Why?

If the speaker has been asked to speak on a certain subject, you may want to mention that. If not, just state that you are sure that what he or she shares "will present a challenge to the group," or "will edify the group" or "will encourage the group."

Receptivity from the Group

Ask for, or state, a desire for receptivity from the group for the speaker. Mention this after you have stated your assurance of the speaker's ability to minister to the group. Paul said to Philemon of Onesimus (Philemon 17) ". . . receive him as you would me."

Welcome the Speaker

Welcome the speaker to the podium both verbally and with your body language. Some suggestions might be a warm embrace, a bow, or a round of applause. The audience will follow your lead and feel the same warmth that you express.

What Else Should I Remember When I Am in Front of a Group?

Besides giving greetings, introductions or formal teachings, there may be other opportunities for you to speak in public. It may be in the form of an inspirational exhortation, a prayer, an announcement or some other significant part of a church service or gathering. Any time that you say something openly in front of an entire congregation or group, you should be willing to ask yourself certain questions. Here is a simple checklist to evaluate your verbal input into a corporate gathering.

1. Have I drawn attention to myself or to the Lord?
2. Will the hearers be able to apply what I have shared to their lives in a practical way?
3. Was my contribution edifying to every listener?
4. What did my words contribute to the service or meeting in a significant way that would have been lacking otherwise?
5. Was it the right time in the order of the service or meeting?
6. Was it redundant? Could I have made it more concise? Was it well prepared and delivered with confidence?
7. What will the hearers remember most? Will they remember the main point of the message, or did my delivery hinder that?

With everything from making a good first impression to critiquing your own public orations, your primary motivating factor should be to honor the Lord and to edify those to whom you are speaking. Do your best to relax, be yourself and trust the Lord.

Chapter 9

COMPASSION

A Servant in Crisis Times

❋

The phone rang and the numbing message came that a young woman, whom I dearly loved, died giving birth to her firstborn son. The shock of this tragedy struck me. Such a thing couldn't happen to this young woman! It seemed that just yesterday she was a student in my Bible college class. She was so talented, so gentle, so unassuming and kind. She was pure, newly married, anxious to be a mother . . . and instantly gone.

Immediate plans needed to be made for how to best minister to the young husband and new father. What should be said? What should be done? Other pastors were at the hospital with him, so meeting at his house with the leaders of his home group seemed to be the next natural step to best assessing the situation.

Upon my arrival at the home, the shocked young widower and new father arrived at the same time. My mind raced for what to say. Each step toward him seemed to linger as I reached up to heaven for words that would offer comfort and express my sorrow. Much to my dismay, out of my mouth popped, "Congratulations on the birth of your firstborn son."

In response, he looked at me with sad eyes that spoke clearly, "I just lost my wife. The son I have, I do not know. The wife I lost, I loved more than words can express. Today I will grieve the death of my wife; tomorrow I will rejoice the life of my new son." Although I felt these words in my spirit, I don't remember if he verbally said anything to me in that moment; he just quietly stepped into his house.

I was immediately horrified, embarrassed and ashamed at my insensitivity to him and to the situation. I wanted to bury myself right there in the front yard. In the midst of my own emotional discomfort, I had jumped over his present sorrow and skipped to his future joy.

A few days later, I reminded him of that moment and asked him to forgive me for my lack of sensitivity and wisdom. He was very gracious and understanding. God had given him grace for the moment in spite of my great lack of wisdom and insight.

Have you ever found yourself in a situation in which you were at a loss for words? Have you ever had a friend in crisis and could offer nothing more than a spiritual platitude? What do you say or do when you don't know what to say or do? What's right? What's wrong? What's sensitive? What's insensitive?

Crisis times are pivotal points in a person's life. Often how a person is ministered to during these times determines whether or not he or she will make it through the ". . . valley of the shadow of death . . ." (Psalm 23:4). The ultimate decision to come through crisis times successfully, of course, belongs to the individual. However, the people surrounding him or her at the time can certainly have a profound effect.

Ministering with perceptive sensitivity to people in crisis is part of the Christian's call. Find encouragement in the fact that God can and will anoint you to do it effectively. Not every crisis situation will end up like my story. If you do have a similar story in your past, humble yourself, repent and learn from it. I have rarely made the same mistake that I made in the previously noted situation.

Ministering to people in crisis situations is required not only for professional ministers of the gospel, but it is also required for every Christian neighbor, friend, co-worker, relative, doctor, nurse and individual who just happens to be there when it occurs. As a Christian woman, you will be required to continually grow in knowledge, wisdom and compassion. If you do not mature in these areas, you will not be able to offer others comfort in this crisis-prone world, and you won't be able to advise others how to offer comfort either.

To be with people in the crisis times of their lives will cost you time, effort, courage and wisdom. Crises generally happen when your schedule is already full to the brim and your energy is running low. It is also not surprising for crises to happen right after you have had a personal stretching experience and feel you're lacking in both wisdom and courage. I know of no other area of ministry that needs more sensitivity and more dependence on the Lord in order to be efficacious than this one.

What Are the Elements of a Crisis?

Every person's response to a crisis is unique. One's personal history, personality and even placement in the family can affect his or her response. The response is also dependent upon a variety of elements within the crisis itself.

Obstacles That Appear to Be Overwhelming

The obstacle could be a problem that would not be serious to most people, but for this individual, it has special significance. Examples of this might be the loss of a job, a sudden geographical move or the loss of a pet.

Obstacles That Appear to Be Cyclical or Unending

Sometimes a person may cope well with short-term problems, but not with long-term situations. Some examples of this would be hormonal problems, long-term debilitating illness or marital separation.

Problems That Occur at a Vulnerable Time

Sometimes the main problem is usually cloaked in a series of minor crises. A problem that a person could normally cope with follows, and he or she loses control because normal coping-mechanisms are not functioning at peak level.

Sudden Shock

Examples of this could be the sudden death of a loved one, the loss of a home due to fire or flooding or the unanticipated birth of a handicapped child.

Giving Birth, Having Surgery or Having Hospital Tests

These situations could be considered elements of a crisis in that they are a shock to the physical body and, in turn, affect the whole person.

The Death of a Loved One

Every individual's grief will be unique, depending on the type of death, the type of person and the placement of the person in the family. The timing of the incident and the nature of the relationship with the deceased may also affect the response. Was the relationship a positive one or a negative one? Was it volatile or was it peaceful? These may be questions that you would want to seek out.

How Do Most People React to Crises?

The most important thing to realize about people in crisis, whatever the specific elements may be, is that in the shock of the moment, most people are frustrated because this is not what they had planned at this time in their lives. They had imagined themselves to be in different situations than those in which they presently find themselves. They probably are not thinking clearly about the present or the future. Suddenly, the present and the future look different than they had imagined–the wheel of life is turning like a kaleidoscope, and they feel a bit unsure.

It is crucial to not confuse this unsurety with a lack of faith in the Lord. Many Christians still have strong faith that the Lord is guiding their steps, they are just temporarily out of sync with their own understanding of His guidance.

There are numerous responses or reactions that people will exhibit during crisis. Knowledge of these may help you not to overreact to hurting people with a quick, spiritual platitude. Their responses may change in the very next sentence. If you toss out a good sounding spiritual platitude too quickly, you may end up sounding like the proverbial fool who has offered an answer before hearing the real problem.

Though responses will be varied and many, some of them may look like this.

Hopelessness or Despair That May Lead to a Sinful Outlet

Perhaps the person in crisis feels that he or she has done something to cause the problem and does not know how to solve it. He or she is full of anxiety and fear and can't do anything to control the circumstances, so he or she turns to drugs, alcohol, anger, escapes into sleep, etc. The list could go on and on. Reality is of course, that the individual can't control the circumstances but can control his or her response to the circumstances.

Physiological or Psychological Symptoms of Stress

Symptoms such as depression, headaches, anxiety attacks, constant worry, ulcers, nervous tension, denial or a resistance to deal with the situation might come into play here.

Shifting the Responsibility to Others

When a person is in crisis, usually he or she first searches for someone to blame. This is part of the normal reasoning process. Whether the individual blames self or someone else, he or she seeks someone or something to blame for the crisis. Finding someone to blame provides a seemingly justifiable reason for what has happened. This, in turn, allows the victim of the crisis to begin making sense of it. Not only will the individual look for someone to blame, but he or she will also tend to look for someone to help relieve the felt pressure. "Doctor, heal me." "Pastor, talk to me." "Family, carry me." These are common themes that you may hear as you minister to people in crisis. Temporarily, these responses are normal. Long-term, they will need to be dealt with and released to the Lord.

Being Unable to Function Normally

The person in the crisis situation still does function, but not at the same pace or with the same efficiency. Decision-making processes may not be as efficient or as logical as they were prior to the crisis. The person may simply move along at a slower pace than he or she used to. Again, this should be a temporary side effect until emotional equilibrium is restored.

These are just a few of the responses or reactions that people may experience in times of crisis. Be aware of them, and be careful to not react to the reaction. Giving people time to sort through their emotions is a reflection of the Christian virtue of grace.

How Can I Help Someone in Crisis?

You may need to provide biblical alternatives to the reactions of those in crisis. However, you must do this by your attitude as well as by your words. The Spirit and the Word offer peace where there is turmoil, love where there is fear and healing where there is wounding. Don't just offer tissue boxes for pity parties, but give genuine compassion cloaked in wisdom.

I'd like to make a few suggestions for ministering to the needs of people in crisis situations.

Be a Listening Ear

People need to be able to acknowledge their losses. They need to be able to talk about what happened and how it has affected them. Some people will want to do this right away, and some will want to do it much later. However, most people do have a distinct need to let it all out at some time. Your responsibility, of course, is to be sensitive to the right timing.

Children, who have lost a sibling or parent to death, may respond with, "I don't want to talk about it." This usually means, "I don't want to have to respond in conversation." If this is the case, inwardly they may desperately long to hear conversation about the deceased or the situation. Similar responses may be heard in divorce situations as well. Children may also have new questions, as they grow older. Ministering to people, who have experienced traumatic, life-altering situations, never really ends in a few days or weeks; it continues as long as the need is there.

People in crisis also need someone else to acknowledge their loss to them. This helps them to adjust to the reality of it. In acknowledging a person's loss, never just say, "I'm sorry." Always follow with a question to which he or she can respond, like "Is there anything I can do to help?" or "How can I pray?" You might say, "I just heard. I'm so sorry. I'm going to stand with you through this. How can I help?" The point is, give the person something to respond to. If you only say, "I'm sorry," then the conversation generally leads the one in grief to comfort you, rather than you comforting him or her.

Never say, "I know just how you feel." No one person knows exactly how another person feels, even though he or she may have experienced a similar loss. It would be more appropriate to say something like, "I'm really feeling with you. I know it was tough for me when I experienced something similar. I'm praying for you." If the individual wants your perspective on it, you've given enough information that the person can ask if he or she wants to. Remember, the goal is to keep the focus on the one in crisis and the Lord, not on you or your experiences in life.

Ask questions that will allow the person in crisis the opportunity to convey his or her needs. For example, if the crisis is an impending surgery, ask if there is a fear of the unknown or of a past negative experience being repeated in the operating room. If the crisis is the birth of a handicapped or terminally ill child, try to discern if there are any self-inflicted judgments. If the crisis is a situation of divorce or the death of a loved one, ask how the relationship was with the lost person in order to discern if there are any emotional regrets. The need that is revealed may not be answerable within the next forty-eight hours, but it may allow you the opportunity to minister again in the near future. Also ask questions that will invite the person to share feelings about his or her present situation, but be careful not to pry inappropriately. Question-asking is important and beneficial, but if there are too many questions, you could heighten the person's anxiety, rather than minister to it.

Be Comforting and Encouraging

This is usually not the time for an exhortation or fresh challenge. Allow the individual to express their grief. This person may express it differently than you would, but you must allow the one in crisis to express it in his or her own way. Some people will weep openly; some will be contemplative. Some cultures weep at births and celebrate at funerals; some weep at funerals and celebrate at births. Some do both in either event. The point is, do not put this person into your prescribed box of do's and don'ts.

Encourage the victim of crisis to allow himself or herself some recovery time. You don't want the person to camp on grief's doorstep, but neither do you want to move the individual along into the next season of life so quickly that he or she doesn't take the time to appropriately grieve the loss. For the loss of a loved one, whether by death or by divorce, it's not uncommon for the process to take a year. The person may not be outwardly grieving everyday for a year, but emotions may surprise him or her throughout that year while facing all of the "firsts" alone (for example, the first anniversary alone, the first birthday alone, the first Valentine's Day alone, the first Thanksgiving alone, the first Christmas alone, etc.).

Most people in traumatic situations go through a series of stages in their grief. Most students of grief recovery agree that some stages tend to be common to most people.

Shock and Disbelief

This is sometimes expressed as, "I don't feel anything" or "I have feelings of nothingness." This is most commonly expressed in the initial phase of grief.

When a child loses a sibling, fear is usually the primary, looming emotion that the child faces. "Will it happen to me?" the child wonders. The next emotion that usually follows is guilt. "It should have been me!" rings in his or her ears. Sitting and talking with a child at the loss of a sibling is crucial. Don't be so engrossed in ministering to the parents that you overlook a tender young plant.

Denial And Isolation

By "denial," I am not indicating that most people actually deny what has happened to them. At least, this hasn't been my experience in working with most Christians. However, I do think that people sometimes put the emotional side of a situation on the shelf in their minds and take it off periodically as they feel they have time or can deal with it.

Some people choose to live with the empty space that the crisis has caused. Some fill up the empty space and replace it with something or someone else, and some ignore the empty space in their hearts and never speak of it again. To walk down memory lane is too painful for them. They don't deny that it happened, but they don't want to talk about it.

Anger

This is usually temporary, and it's best just to allow people to process it through with the Lord. However, anger can occasionally turn into bitterness, resentment and backsliding. When that happens, pick up your "Sword," the Word of God, and surgically remove the hard shell without wounding the heart of flesh inside.

Guilt and Bargaining With God

This stage of grief may result in prayers like this: "God, if you'll heal my husband, I'll never complain again. I'll even be willing to serve you in the far reaches of the earth."

Depression

At this stage, it's important for people to know that it's okay to cry. Usually, the person left in charge of the family or the firstborn child carries the burden of the crisis. Because this person carries the responsibility, he or she often feels that an emotional breakdown would leave no one for the rest of the family to lean on. This person literally sacrifices himself or herself emotionally for the sake of the rest of the family. Obviously, someone does need to be in charge during times of crisis. However, if this person refuses to step aside and deal with his or her own emotions, it can cause depression later.

Also, some people refuse depression and simply freeze up emotionally. They block their tears and ignore the empty space inside. This will not necessarily hinder them, unless the locking up of their emotions stifles their normal emotional growth in other areas.

Acceptance

Though the grieving person must reconcile with God over the loss, he or she may always feel partial emptiness inside in regard to this loss. He or she may also come to accept the fact that there are no explanations as to why the crisis has occurred. The individual has accepted the fact that regardless of the circumstances, God loves him or her and He still has everything under His sovereign rule.

Healing and Restored Faith

This is not to say that every person will lose faith as he or she experiences loss in life. However, as the storms of life come, sometimes one's confidence in his or her faith needs to be restored. When wounding comes through loss, healing definitely comes as a blessing from the Lord. At this stage, people are ready to continue on in the journey. They may walk with a limp as Jacob did, as referred to in chapter four, but they do walk.

Not every person will go through these stages. Some people will go through each stage like clockwork. Some people will go through a few of the stages, and some will not go through any of them. It's important that you do not try to force people to go through each of these stages, as you may hurt them in the process. It's also crucial that you don't accuse people of being in denial if they do not go through these common stages. If they are in some form of denial, patience and compassion will help them, not accusation and unveiling. Sometimes the Lord does give a person supernatural acceptance of their loss and an immediate joy and trust in Him. If that is his or her confession, be grateful, and don't predict a nervous breakdown in a few months. Let God be God–He is so much better at it.

Verbalize Acceptance of the Person in Crisis

People mourn the loss of anything that is precious to them, whether a pet, a grandparent or a home. Never minimize a person's loss or try to diminish the feelings that he or she is having. Don't compare this person's grief to someone else's experience. In the same week, one family may lose a home to fire, and another family may lose a child in a car accident. Your temptation may be to minimize the loss of the home when comparing it to the loss of the child. That would lack the compassion and wisdom of Christ. Allow people to be wherever they are in the healing process without bringing shame to them through the avenue of comparison.

Do Not Try to Answer the "Whys"

Simply direct the one in crisis to "Who" will help him or her through it. Often on this side of heaven, there are no answers to the "why" questions in times of crisis. People may ask you to answer why a child dies from cancer, why a friend is brutally raped and murdered, why a leader violates a teen or why a church building or family business is burned to the ground. However, why innocent people suffer is, indeed, a mystery that only God Himself can answer. In these difficult, seeming contradictions let people ask the questions of their hearts, but gently direct them to the One who will help them to get through this difficult season. Only Jesus can heal their hearts.

Make a list of scriptural promises to have readily available when necessary. Memorize some key scriptures of hope and comfort. Write them in the back of your Bible. Be prepared to give a word of hope whenever needed.

How Can I Offer Practical Assistance to Those in Crises?

Matthew 25:40 says, ". . . inasmuch as you did it to one of the least of these My brethren, you did it to me." Jesus spoke these words in relation to demonstrating compassion to the hungry, thirsty, lonely, naked and sick. He challenges us to deeply realize, through this parable, that His people are truly His Body. When we minister to one another, we minister to Him. This is quite a revelation to grasp!

Of course, there are many ways to do this. Every way in which we serve is significant, from serving in a soup kitchen for the poor, to visiting a person in prison or ministering to those with a recent loss.

Hospital Visitation

Hospital visitation is one of the ways you may be called upon to minister to people and fulfill Matthew 25:40. Sadly, in many churches, this has become a lost ministry. Hospital visitation is one of the most wonderful opportunities to actively demonstrate the love of Christ, not only to the sick person, but also to family members and to others nearby. It is also one of the easiest places to share the gospel of Jesus Christ with the lost.

Of course, there are a variety of reasons for which people are admitted to the hospital–some for the joy of a baby's birth, some for surgery or the setting of broken bones, some for dialysis, transplants or cancer treatments. Some come for a short stay; some are admitted long-term. Whatever the reason or the length of the hospital stay, let me offer a few practical suggestions for an appropriate visit.

Prepare Emotionally

Be emotionally prepared, before you enter the hospital room, for what the person may look like. If you've never visited someone in a coma or after surgery, I recommend that you go along with someone who has, and visit someone who you are not emotionally attached to. A look of shock from a visitor will assure the patient that he or she is worse off than originally thought.

Smile

Smile as you enter the room. Do your best to look confident and emanate the Lord's faith in the situation.

Touch the Patient

Touch the patient gently in some way. Encouragement comes to all of us through physical affection. Scripture tells us to ". . . lay hands on the sick, and they will recover" (Mark 16:18). There is healing in a touch. Touch the person's hand or leg when you pray or talk to him or her. However, be careful not to be over exuberant. Do not touch the surgery zone or one of the cords attached to the patient-you don't want to cut off the oxygen supply! Also be careful not to step on any cords.

Pray

Pray for the patient or read a scripture. If you read a scripture, write the reference on a card and leave it for the patient to meditate on later. Be sure that it is a comforting scripture, not one that exhorts or condemns. This can be very spiritually bonding between you and that person.

Be Sensitive About the Time

Don't stay long unless the patient has specifically requested for you to do so.

Bring Flowers or a Gift

Bring flowers or a plant and leave a card so that the patient will know that you were there. Sometimes people will be awake and carry on a conversation immediately following surgery, but they won't remember it the next day, due to post-surgery medication. Sometimes patients will be asleep when you arrive. If they are, don't wake them! Generally, people in hospitals need rest for their bodies. Simply leave a card indicating that you were there.

Some possible gift ideas would be a robe, slippers, perfume, cologne, powder, lotion, mild-flavored candies, magazines, instrumental audio cassettes or note cards. For extended recovery times, a book, a teaching cassette, a facial, a manicure, a pedicure, etc.

Call on the Phone

If you are unable to physically visit, a phone call is appropriate and certainly better than ignoring the patient altogether. If you call, be brief, positive and caring. Do not call every day, unless you want to offer a scripture for that day's meditation or to extend a brief prayer. If you do plan to do something like this, it is best to ask the patient when would be the best time of the day for this short call.

Don't Take Small Children

Do not take small children along unless the patient has specifically requested it. You will not be as relaxed in conversation if you need to keep your eye on your child. The patient may also become uneasy if the child starts to wander around the room and get curious about the hospital apparatus, even though you may be chirping away like a carefree bird enjoying your visit. Also, small children tend to look terrified at how differently the patient may look to them. This would not be an endearing moment for your child or for the patient. If you feel that you cannot leave your child to make the visit, don't stay home. Ask a teen to go along with you and stay with the child in the waiting room while you run in for a brief visit.

After a Hospital Stay or the Death of a Loved One

Sometimes, considerations should be made for people before and after a hospital stay or after the death of a loved one. The main key to success in this arena will be communication. Simply, ask the person how you could best help them. There is no need to serve people in ways that they really would prefer not to be served. Here are a few possibilities.

Provide Meals

If hospitalized, the patient's family may need help with meals before he or she returns home, especially if the wife or mother is hospitalized.

In the case of a birth or surgery, arrange for one week of meals. Then ask if the family may need this service longer. They may not need it until after a helping relative leaves town a week or two later.

When there is a death in the family, arrange meals from the time of death through the funeral day. Then ask the family if they would like to receive meals for a few more days. Leaving funeral dinner leftovers in non-returnable containers may be a good idea. Again, ask the family's preference.

When planning menus over an extended period, be sure to ask what the family favorites are. Then arrange for people to bring different menus each day. The family shouldn't have to eat the same main course three evenings in a row. Keep in mind that new mothers, who are breast-feeding babies, and post-surgery patients cannot easily handle foods that are spicy or rich, like garlic, onion, broccoli, chocolate, etc.

Household Chores

Vacuuming, dusting and mopping floors are all good ways to help someone in an extended recovery situation. Offering to do laundry, at least the bedding and towels, can also be helpful as surgery patients should not be lifting heavy loads of clothes during their recovery phase.

Do not take small children with you to help. You will accomplish your tasks more quickly without them, and you won't make the recovering patient nervous, wondering where the child is wandering while you are working in another room.

Yard Work

Mowing the grass or weeding the flowerbeds can be especially encouraging and helpful to an elderly person, who has recently lost a mate or had surgery or cancer treatments. Getting teens involved in this ministry can be fun and quick work.

Grocery Shopping

For extended surgery recoveries, going grocery shopping for the recovering patient or offering to take him or her shopping while you do all the lifting and carrying can be very helpful and encouraging.

Other Considerations When a Death in the Family Has Occurred

Help provide or organize transportation and lodging arrangements for out-of-town family members. Offer baby-sitting services for small children during the funeral service. Check with the widow or widower concerning clothing, and see if anything needs to be cleaned for the funeral or memorial service. If there is no extended family to assist, ask if the individual would like assistance with rearranging a room or pictures of the deceased. Help locate an experienced photographer for the family at the funeral. Make sure notepads and pens are near each telephone in the house. Get obituary notices from newspapers for the family. Depending on the situation, you may need to offer to help write the obituary.

Help the Partner of the Deceased to Adjust Back Into His or Her Normal Life Pattern

Again, communication is the main key to success here. Ask the individual how you can best help.

Ask if he or she would like to sit with you in church, or if you could save seats for the family wherever they would prefer. Make sure that they have needed transportation.

Ask if the person needs help cleaning out a room. Of course, be sensitive here. Most people have family members who will do this, and it may be offensive if you offer. However, for someone who has no family, this may be appropriate if you have a close relationship.

Ask if the partner of the deceased is financially secure. Again, this would depend upon the involvement of the extended family. If he or she has no family, ask if any assistance with paperwork of insurance, funeral bills, etc. is needed. If so, find a trusted person, professional or lawyer to help.

Several weeks or months later, it would be good to bring up the deceased person in conversation and give the partner an opportunity to talk. You might also ask how other family members are handling the loss. This helps him or her to realize that you have not forgotten the deceased. It also helps him or her verbalize feelings at this time.

What Should Be My Heart Attitude?

Acts 20:35 says, ". . . It is more blessed to give than to receive." Giving out the love that God has so graciously given is definitely blessed. As you give out of an unselfish heart, you'll be amazed at the rewards that will return to you. However, never let rewards be your motivation. If you do you probably will miss the hidden treasures that will come your way.

Recently I visited Kalaupapa, the home of those who were stricken with leprosy many years ago. It is now a national park on the Hawaiian Island of Molokai. The tour guide for our group had been a victim of leprosy before a cure was discovered in the 1940s. At the age of fourteen, along with his six-year-old brother, he was banished to the island to die. The brothers each had ring worm on their arms, and it was misdiagnosed as leprosy. After being placed on the island with the more than six hundred victims of leprosy, they contracted the disease.

The tour guide married a young woman who had also been sent there with a misdiagnosis. (Numerous others in the colony had been misdiagnosed as well, due to tremendous fear of the disease at that time.) This couple soon had two children. When babies were born on the island, they were immediately taken from the mother and sent to another island. If the extended family did not want them, due to the shame that was connected with leprosy, they would be sent to orphanages. The children of our tour guide were both taken in and raised by their grandparents. He showed us a picture of his first grandchild with pride in his eyes.

Many times throughout the tour, our guide spoke of how grateful he was for those who came so many years ago, before there was a cure, and ministered love and compassion to them, "the great outcasts of the world."

As this articulate, kind gentleman shared his story, I asked, "How did you deal with the injustice of being misdiagnosed and then contracting leprosy as a teen?" Without any hint of resentment or bitterness in his voice, he said, "I believe that God makes no mistakes." The message he delivered that day, through his manner, as well as through his speech, was the importance of compassion–compassion that is not only spoken of but is demonstrated.

The people who went to the island to minister to those with leprosy in the late 1800s and the early 1900s had no cure to offer but love and compassion. The Catholic priest, Father Damien, was the first to minister to these people. His testimony is incredible. On his monument in Hawaii is engraved the scripture, "Greater love hath no man than this, that a man lay down his life for his friends" (John 15:13, KJV). As we minister to others, may this message of Christ ring, not only in our spirits, but also through our actions daily.

SECTION THREE:

❋

your
Relationships

Chapter 10

TEAMWORK
A Member of the Team

A very significant part of accomplishing the calling that God has placed in your own heart will involve teamwork with others. God has created each of us in such a way as to have a need, not only for Him, but for others as well. To have proficient teamwork, each member of the team must function unselfishly and within the realms of his or her individual gifts, talents and callings. Each member of the team is valuable and needed.

If you lack understanding of the importance and value of the team, you may lack clear vision and busy yourself with climbing the social, ministerial or business ladder solely for the sake of getting to the top. Sadly, climbing these kinds of ladders often involves stepping on others along the way. If you do so, you may find that the rungs will fall out from beneath you when you have reached the pinnacle of your destination.

Whether you are at the top, bottom, or somewhere in between in your place of ministry or employment, you'll be at the top of God's ladder if you are obedient to His personal calling and placement in your life. This is not to say that if you're functioning in a supportive role today, you won't be in a senior or supervisory role in the future. However, it is in God's calling and placement that you will find His anointing.

Am I Fulfilling My Primary Function?

I believe that there are many gifted people who are functioning poorly in their positions as senior leaders because their primary gifting is in a supportive role. There are also many people who are functioning in supportive roles who are actually hiding behind that role instead of courageously stepping up to bat in a primary leadership role. This mismatching occurs in businesses, pastorates and small committees as well. It occurs, not only in large corporations, but also in church musicals and neighborhood Boy Scout programs.

This scenario is like the child who tries to fit the square peg into the round hole, or the person who continually looks over the fence and thinks, "The grass is greener on the other side." When people do this for too long, they jump over the fence and then wonder how the grass got brown so quickly. They feel maladjusted and claim that they just don't fit anymore.

When this happens, people begin to look for someone to blame. They often blame others on the team, the senior pastor or supervisor who seemingly doesn't see their gifts. They may blame their mates or their children for holding them back or for pushing them ahead too soon. They look for someone to blame for their wrong motivations, and suddenly, other people get hurt.

Just as a comparative few will have the gifts or callings to be senior pastors or presidents of corporations, many will have the gifts to lead in some area of support. Hence, there are fewer senior positions than there are support opportunities. Whichever position you are called to function in, accept that position with joy. One position is not more important than the other. From God's perspective, one group is not elite over the other.

This is especially true within the Body of Christ. How or where you function in the church setting does not equate to your personal value to God. Any seasoned and wise corporate executive knows this to be true in business as well. Each person who functions in his or her unique capacity is valuable to the bigger picture.

My husband once heard of a senior pastor who had pastored a couple of churches, rather unsuccessfully, from his own perspective. One day he received a request to come and pastor a small church in another city and felt the prompting from the Lord to do so. Within a few short years of his arrival, the church had grown until the congregation was quite large and there were several support ministers on staff.

One day, a senior citizen in the congregation phoned and asked the church secretary if the pastor would come and visit her in the hospital. The pastor, being very busy yet very caring, sent one of the other staff pastors to visit her. She sincerely thanked him for coming, told him that she knew that she was going to die soon and requested earnestly that the senior pastor come to see her.

Upon hearing this, the senior pastor went to see her in the hospital. As he entered the room, he recognized her as a woman who was faithful in attendance, but one who generally sat quietly toward the back of the congregation. The woman graciously thanked him for coming. She then told him that she knew she was going to die soon and that she had one request to make of him. She began to earnestly request that he find someone to take her place of ministry in the church. Rather embarrassed, he assured her that he would do so but admitted that he was unsure of what her ministry was in the church.

She then began to tell her story. She told him how, after he had first arrived as the pastor, she had prayed and asked the Lord what her ministry was to be in the church. She said that the Lord told her that He wanted her to spend every Saturday night in prayer for the pastor and his ministry on Sunday morning. She said that she had been faithful to fulfill the Lord's calling all these years and now she felt such urgency that someone needed to take her place of ministry in the Body.

The pastor suddenly realized what had made the difference between his previous two pastoral experiences and this current one, which had blossomed so quickly for no apparent reason other than the Lord's favor. Can you imagine how he felt at that moment? I think his inner response was something like this: "Don't die on me now, lady!"

Who was really responsible for impacting that church and that city for Christ, the intercessor or the pastor? Both, of course. She did what the Lord asked of her and he did what the Lord asked of him. Each was essential. One position could not function effectively without the other. Each needed to be functioning in order for the other to function.

Whatever your call, realize that every member of the Body is important and vital. One is not superior over the other, nor is one inferior to the other. True servants of the Lord know this and are thankful for the functioning of each member of the Body. Whether you are called to be the senior leader or the intercessor, do your part for the glory of God and His purposes in the earth.

Let promotion come from the Lord, and remember that mankind is impressed with titles while God is impressed with obedience. It will be your own pride, false concepts or emotion-led reasoning that will cause you to look for promotion, rather than placement. If you have a wrong perspective, you will be easily influenced by others' opinions of your position. God-ordained placement brings lasting fulfillment, not promotion that comes from man.

What Misconceptions Confront Those in Leadership Roles?

Senior leaders and supervisors are often seen as being out to lift up their own names and to build up their own kingdoms, so to speak. Some are seen as having all wisdom and being superior to others on the team. Some are seen as being too busy, untouchable or unreachable. Some are seen as not having any needs. None of these perspectives are true of humble servants of God and should never be true of you, if you are called to this type of position.

Leaders in supportive positions are sometimes seen as being second best. Their positions are viewed as stepping-stones to senior leadership. Sadly, some see supportive leadership as "just a job," rather than a true vocation or ministry. Some feel that those in supportive leadership are less qualified than those in senior leadership. Again, none of these perspectives are true of humble servants of God and should never be true of you, if you are called to this type of position.

Even though you may be functioning in a supportive capacity, you may also be functioning in a primary leadership role. For example, you may be a senior supervisor over a group of section supervisors, yet you are under the direction of the vice-president of the company. Perhaps you are the youth pastor over a group of teen small group leaders, yet you are accountable to the senior pastor of the church. You may be the head of a Sunday school department, yet you give regular reports to the super-intendent. Wherever you function, you may find that you function in a dual capacity, both as a senior leader and in a supportive position.

Whether you are functioning primarily in the church or in the workplace, as a Christian woman of influence, you have a responsibility to handle your roles appropriately. You may be a supervisor on your job and a supportive team member in a small group in the church. You may be a senior pastor and an assistant coach for the neighborhood soccer team. Real life usually carries with it such variety. Please allow me to offer a few suggestions for handling leadership in each of these scenarios, senior leadership and the supportive leadership.

What are the Challenges of a Senior Leader?

Giving the Primary Direction

The leadership team often will not step out and voice an opinion concerning direction until they first hear it from you, their senior leader. The workers under you or the congregation will also wait to hear the trumpet call from you before they will be motivated to serve or give to a cause.

Disagreeing with the Leadership Team

When you feel that the Lord is urgently speaking on a matter, yet you're unable to come to agreement with your supporting leadership team on it, you must discern the Lord's will in terms of timing and your presentation of the issue at hand.

Remaining Loyal to the Leadership Team

Do not yield yourself to the temptation to gossip about members of your supporting leadership team when you are frustrated with them, when they are not in agreement with you or when they are not being all that they should be in their serving. This kind of action belittles them personally and belittles their leadership in the eyes of those to whom you are speaking.

Belittling another will never validate your leadership. Gossip may be cathartic in the beginning, but it will demean your own leadership in the long run. People will have less respect for you because of your gossip.

However, they will respect you more for being loyal. Getting needed perspective from another senior leader concerning an individual or team issue is different than exposing a team member to a peer.

When you are in a position of leadership, everything you say will be repeated. Plan on it! Also, know that it will always be repeated with a slant. Be careful to slant what you say in a positive light, so that when it is repeated it is already headed in the right direction.

Developing Friendships with Other Members of the Leadership Team

Accept the fact that you will never be able to please everyone when it comes to choosing your friends. However, doing your best to be friendly and hospitable will mean a lot to everyone. As Proverbs 18:24 says, "A man who has friends must himself be friendly . . ." Developing friendships with your supporting leadership team could save you much duress at a later time when the enemy is attacking you, your time schedule or your reputation.

Dealing with Time Pressure

Some people will expect you to counsel with them or pray with them at all hours of the day or night. Others will expect you to take time off and have lunch with them or go shopping with them just for the fun of it. They will accuse you of being unreachable or untouchable if you don't meet their demands.

Settle for yourself the fact that other people have no concept of how your schedule functions. Neither do they realize how long it takes to prepare a sermon, do a meaningful hospital visitation or absorb the details and considerations of company projects. Most people do not mean to be uncaring or inconsiderate, they simply feel honored when you give them some of your time.

Work hard at remaining grateful for the people in your life that care about you. At the same time, learn to balance your work schedule and take time off without feeling guilty. God created the Sabbath rest day for leaders as much as He did for others. Your day off may not be on the same day as everyone else, but you still need one.

Receiving Personal Criticism

Receive criticism graciously, and then take it to the Lord for evaluation. Have another trusted and wise person, to whom you have given permission, speak into your life on the issue. That person may be a spouse or another person in a senior leadership position. After taking the criticism to the Lord, take it to this objective sounding board and ask his or her perspective. If both agree that the criticism is justified, then humbly make the necessary adjustment. If not, move on.

Don't let the enemy berate you at times like these. Remember, no one is perfect.

Receiving Criticism About Members of the Leadership Team

When a person begins to speak critically of someone else, ask the person bringing the criticism if he or she has personally spoken with the team member who is the object of criticism. If not, direct this person to do so. If the person has already confronted the team member on the subject, then ask him or her about the response of the team member, and find out if there are any other accusers. Then, assure the person that you have heard what he or she has said and will consider it carefully. Next, reassure him or her of the accused team member's integrity and godly motivation. Speak with the accused of the concern. When doing so, assure them of your belief in his or her integrity and place on the team.

Handle the situation as you would like it to be handled if you were the one being criticized. Always believe the best of your team members. Promoting faith in their leadership fosters honesty and humility in them. If they do need adjustment, let truth and grace be in your words and do it with precision and kindness. You may need this grace returned someday.

Maintaining Perspective While Handling Details

While keeping a firm grip on the broader picture, be aware of necessary details in individual departments. It is not necessary to know every detail of every department in the church or the company. However, it is important to have leaders, whom you trust, in each department to handle situations and make decisions in the same manner as you would before the Lord.

You are responsible to keep abreast of enough details in each department that you can make the best decisions for all who are affected. Be sure to keep sight of the big picture. In other words, your job is to be sure that the right hand always knows what the left hand is doing. However, don't be overly influenced by one department.

Keeping Proper Demeanor and Behavior in Relationships

The manner in which you relate to others will be the same manner in which your other team leaders will evaluate what is appropriate for their behavior. Never act in any way that would cause your spouse, or anyone else, one moment of doubt concerning your motive toward another person. Actions that might cause doubt could be anything from sensual innuendoes to tones of irritation and resentment. It is important to handle people with the same purity and care that Christ would.

Again, your leadership team will tend to follow suit. You could easily see your shortcomings multiplied in others through your leadership team. Be careful. Leviticus 11:44 says, ". . . consecrate yourselves, and you shall be holy; for I am holy. . . ."

Accepting Little or No Salary

Salary would probably not be an issue in a large corporation. However, if you have your own small business or are in the ministry, you may receive a very low salary. As the senior leader, you may work many hours in the church and receive no financial remuneration. This is not the case for all small businesses and congregations, but for some, it is a painful reality.

If you are leading a church, be sure that you are teaching the congregation biblical principles of tithing and giving offerings to the Lord. However, when you do this, be careful to do it for the sake of the congregation and not for your own benefit. Be sure to tithe and give offerings yourself. Don't complain to individual people in hopes that they will bless you. This dishonors the Lord.

Keep the Lord as your banker. Hold the Lord accountable to provide your needs while you function in the area of your calling. Of course, you may receive a salary through the church or business, but the Lord will always be the one you look to as your provider. If you do this, you'll cultivate an attitude of gratitude that the Lord will bless.

In the church world, people may expect you to dress like a queen but only allow you money enough to shop at the second hand store. If this is the case, find the best dressed, second hand store shopper in the church and ask her to teach you how to shop. If this is not your preference, then purchase quality, not quantity, or learn to sew. However you manage your budget, don't allow Satan to make you bitter. God is storing up your unrewarded service and your gratefulness in the heavens. He sees. He knows.

If you are sincerely losing your grace for this, ask yourself a few questions: "Is this what I am really called to do?" "Should I work at another job for a season to help out financially?" "Is my family being hurt and becoming embittered by this?" "Is my faith in God, or am I seeing only the storm?"

What are the Challenges of the Supporting Leader?

Dealing with Inappropriate Pressure for Promotion

Others will constantly ask and wonder when you are going to move up. Resist the temptation to view your present place of calling as a mere stepping stone. Embracing this viewpoint would be using God's present calling for your own selfish benefit. It is belittling to those with whom you presently work and it definitely is not pleasing to the Heavenly Father.

God will always desire to use your present circumstance to groom you for the future. However, He also wants you to live in the present. He wants you to fully experience all that He has for you now. If you continually look over the fence at the next step, you will miss what He has for you now. There are lessons in the present situation.

Yielding to inappropriate promotion pressure can stir up frustration, wrong motivation and untimely changes. It is not wrong to have a vision for something more, but it is wrong to resist the position in which the Lord has placed you. Never forget that function does not equal value.

Disagreeing with the Senior Leader or Supervisor

Satan is not always the author of disagreement, but he loves to use it to his advantage. Watch out for this. You may feel that you have a word from the Lord on a matter with which the senior leader does not agree. Submission does not mean stifling your perspective, but it does mean that once you've given it, you need to offer it up to the Lord and trust the anointing He has placed on the office of the senior leader.

Realize the influence that you have on the supporting team, and don't be disloyal. If you disagree with the senior leader, ask yourself a few questions: "Is my ego tied to my opinion?" "Did I present my position with clarity and in a godly manner that was able to be received?" "Is this the right time?" "In the long run, does it really matter?" Never hesitate to check your own motives before judging another.

Also, remember that the senior leader is responsible to consider the bigger picture and may see things from a different perspective for a specific reason. His or her reasoning may not seem logical to you, but it may be very logical to God.

Remaining Loyal to the Senior Leader

As with the senior leader on this issue, you must not yield yourself to the temptation to gossip when you are frustrated. This kind of action belittles not only the leader personally, but also the office of the senior leader. You could seriously hinder his or her ability to effectively lead the congregation or the business.

Once again, belittling another will never validate your leadership in the congregation or the corporation. Although others may incite or encourage disloyal comments at the outset, in the long run, people will always respect you more for being loyal.

Just as with the senior leader, know that everything you say will be repeated. Plan on it! However, also know that your words will always be repeated with the hearer's perspective in mind. Be careful to slant whatever you say in a positive manner, so that when it is repeated, it is already headed in the right direction.

If you have a serious concern with the leadership skills of the person in charge, carefully follow the procedures prescribed in Matthew eighteen, and confront him or her privately. If you are not received and two or three others, who bear witness, also have not been received, then share your concern with someone to whom he or she is accountable, but never gossip among other employees or church members. Gossip is definitely not a Christian testimony.

Developing Friendships with the Senior Leader and Other Members of the Leadership Team

The key is to be the kind of friend to the senior leader that he or she needs you to be. Do not go into a relationship with a lot of expectations.

If you are a generation younger than your supervisor or senior pastor, accept the fact that though you may be a special daughter in the Lord, you'll never have the same relationship as the leader's own blood-born sons and daughters. (There may be some exceptions to this, of course.)

If you are more of a peer to your boss or senior pastor, realize that you may never be counted as one of his or her very closest confidants. You'll have a better chance of becoming close if you don't put pressure on him or her by expecting that closeness.

If your senior leader is younger than you, don't mother him or her. God has placed this person in an office that you are to revere, as you would your physician, a police officer or the president.

Handling Time Pressure

You will have many of the same time pressures and expectations from friends, family, and those under you, that the boss or senior pastor does. However, you will also have the pressure of your schedule not really being your own.

While doing your best to make your senior leader a success, you must also fulfill your obligations to your own job description. Just realize that part of your job description is to be responsive and helpful to the senior leader when you're needed, and to not be envious and complaining when you're not needed. This will be challenging at times. You'll be stretched, but you will be blessed!

Receiving Personal Criticism and Criticism About the Senior Leader and Other Members of the Leadership Team

What I have written on this area under the senior leader section would apply here also. The rule of thumb is to handle people with grace and wisdom.

Maintaining Perspective While Handling Details

While keeping a firm grip on the details of your individual department, be aware of the bigger picture. You don't need to know every detail of every department, but you do need to know enough about each area that you could give a newcomer a general idea of what is involved in each department.

For example, in the church world, if the janitor is responsible for lost Bibles, you need to know who he is and how someone can get in touch with him. If someone wants to join the choir, you need to know who the choir director is. If someone wants to volunteer for children's ministry, you need to know who the children's pastor is. If someone is hosting a banquet for the newlyweds of the church, you may need to be able to tell them who to contact to get a key to the kitchen. In other words, you need to stay abreast of the basics.

You also need to know some of these details in order to maintain a broad perspective of the church or the business as a whole. Working at this will help you to better understand your supervisor or senior pastor's responsibility and perspective. It will also give you a better working relationship with other leaders on the team and help you to make decisions as a team. The larger a church or corporation becomes, the more challenging this becomes, but it still needs to be done.

Keeping Proper Demeanor and Behavior in Relationships

As with the senior leader, you should never act in any way that would cause your spouse, or anyone else, one moment of doubt concerning your motive toward another person. This doubt could be caused by anything from sensual innuendoes to tones of irritation and resentment. You also must handle people with the same purity and care that Christ would.

As a supportive leader, always act appropriately toward your supervisor or senior pastor. Never appear to be overly familiar with your leader or allow inappropriate anger to flare up toward him or her. This person is your leader and should be treated with respect, even though you may become very close, intimate friends.

As a woman, you should never allow yourself to become flirtatious or too intimate in behavior or conversation with a male pastor or boss. Always think of him as someone's spouse, as "the two have become one." If he comes to you for counsel concerning a personal marital issue, respectfully, but firmly, direct him to a brother in the Lord. Do not allow yourself to spend large amounts of time with him privately, working on company or church projects. You should not work overtime hours with him alone on a consistent basis. If there is occasion for this for a season, request that other volunteers be brought in to aid in the project at hand.

These same principles would apply to any other male leaders on the team. Of course, if you or others on the team have had any prior lesbian involvement, the same precautions should be made with other female leaders as well. The key is to be wise, not naïve.

Accepting Little or No Salary

In the church world, as a supportive minister, you may receive no financial remuneration for your services, yet work just as hard and just as many hours as the senior pastor. You may have been hired to work on the church staff, but you receive a lower salary than the senior pastor, even though you may feel that you carry the same ministry weight.

Any senior pastor, who was once a supportive minister, or any boss, who was once an employee, would tell you that though the work hours might be the same, the pressure definitely is not. The full weight of the responsibility is difficult to understand if you've never been the main person in charge. Yes, you will have pressure, but it's not the same.

Some of what you perceive in this area may be accurate, and some may not be. Whether you receive what seems to be a comparable salary or not, you need to keep a faith attitude. Satan loves to trip up God's servants in this area. Accept the fact that, in a supportive position, you will never receive the same salary as the senior leader does. Don't allow Satan to pull you down into a fruitless, comparison mindset.

In the church world, you may need to accept the fact that you must live on a small salary all or most of your life. This is not the case in all churches, but in many, it is. The larger the church staff is, the more the finances need to be spread out. The more the finances are spread out, the less there is for each individual.

Although your salary may be low, people will still expect you to dress as well as the senior leader does. Learning how to dress like a princess on a pauper's wage is a real talent! Jesus loves to help.

To handle this in faith, know your personal priorities and your personal call. When you know this, you'll rejoice in it because your financial provision will no longer come from the church, but from the Lord. He delights to bless His children who walk in faith. You will find that you cannot out-give the Lord. He will bless you in ways that will go beyond your imagination.

As mentioned before, if you are presently living on a low salary and are losing the grace for it, ask yourself a few questions: "Am I called to do this?" "Could I do this and work another job without hurting my family and the people for whom I am responsible?" "Was this calling for a season of time that I am no longer in?" "Am I afraid to change vocations?"

How Can I Do My Best as a Team Member?

Wise and humble senior leaders, supervisors, employees and volunteers all realize that, in the church world, unity is essential. All positions are merely places of function within the Body of Christ. All positions will come to their completion at the return of Jesus Christ. Fruit will be measured and obedience will be rewarded, not function or ministry position.

There simply is not enough time for the members of Christ's Church to be fussing over who does what. This kind of bickering was never okay with the Lord in the past, and it certainly is not okay now. Each member is needed and is important. Not only is it God's will for you to be an excellent employee, but it's also His will for you to find your place of function in the church, rejoice in it and go for it wholeheartedly.

Romans 12:9-14 says, "Let love be without hypocrisy. Abhor what is evil. Cling to what is good. Be kindly affectionate to one another with brotherly love, in honor giving preference to one another; not lagging in diligence, fervent in spirit, serving the Lord; rejoicing in hope, patient in tribulation, continuing steadfastly in prayer; distributing to the needs of the saints, given to hospitality. Bless those who persecute you; bless and do not curse." May each of us, as Christian women of influence, fulfill this passage of Scripture as we function in our jobs and in our homes, as well as in our ministries.

Chapter 11

FRIENDSHIP
A Woman of Many Friends

❋

There are many books on the topic of friendship on the market today. My goal, in this chapter, is not to give you one more lesson on friendship, but rather to reach into your perspective and speak heart-to-heart. Many Christian women have studied this topic and can teach it with great passion, but the actual practicing of it eludes them more times than they care to admit. It remains a personal mystery that baffles the soul and brings the sting of loneliness to their quiet moments.

As you study Scripture on this subject, it seems that this scenario should be just the opposite of our experience. The word "friend(s)" is used over one hundred times in the Bible, from Genesis to III John. The pattern for friendship is found in David and Jonathan, Ruth and Naomi, and Jesus and his disciples. David was a leader, Naomi was a prominent woman, and Jesus was certainly an influential person.

The patterns for friendship are there for us in Scripture. Why does it slip through the fingers so easily? Why does it leave women near the phone, hoping someone will call who doesn't just want advice or a new recipe idea, but wants friendship? Why do many women look out over the sea of humanity and observe others enjoying the fruit of friendship, yet have only the illusion of it working in their own lives?

Why Is It Important That I Have Friends?

God designed us with an awareness of our need for relationships. In Genesis 2:20, as soon as Adam realized that there was ". . . not found a helper comparable to him," God put him to sleep and created a friend to walk through life with him. If you haven't read Genesis one and two for a while, read these chapters again. Notice that God does not create Eve until Adam becomes aware of his need. Are you aware of your personal need?

There are a variety of reasons that relationships will end or change over the years, but never forget that God did create you with a need for companionship. God did it. This need is not some weakness in your personality, but rather something that God put in your heart.

In the busyness of our varied responsibilities, sometimes we get used to being alone and are not even aware of the need for friends. You may be tempted to rationalize at times, "Friendships take time that I simply do not have to give." In reality, I think that this rationalization is from the author of lies, Satan himself. Many things that Satan will have to say to you over the years will be very logical and have elements of truth. Friendships do take time, and you are busy. (I think that we live in the busiest era of time that has ever been.) However, if you don't take time to cultivate friendships in the busyness of harvest time, you could be lonely when winter comes. In winter, aloneness can turn into loneliness.

Even nature speaks to us of our need for friends. The sequoia trees of California, which grow as tall as three hundred feet, have unusually shallow root systems. Their roots reach out in all directions in order to receive the greatest amount of surface moisture. Because of this, rarely will a great sequoia tree stand alone, as strong winds could easily uproot it. Rather, the trees intertwine their roots with other nearby trees providing support for one another against storms.

We all have winter seasons in our lives. We all have storms to face. Sometimes, your help in times of trouble will be God alone, and other times, it will be friends that He has placed strategically in your life ". . . for such a time as this" (Esther 4:14).

When Esther was in her season of challenge, she needed friends to fast and pray with her, friends to stand with her. If she hadn't cultivated friendships previous to her trial, perhaps she wouldn't have succeeded. Not only did a nation of strangers go on a national fast with her, but also her maidens. She didn't select the garment to wear as she appeared before the king; this task went to Hegai, her mentor. Her own discernment or knowledge did not bring the challenge to save a nation; this wisdom came from her family member, Mordecai. Just as Esther cultivated a variety of friendships, so must you.

What are My Differing Roles in Friendships?

A wise woman will not look at friendships merely in dresser drawer fashion. She will not limit herself to seeing her friends only in levels, such as intimate, close, casual and acquaintance. These are not necessarily unrealistic categories, but they become very limiting if they are the only options.

A close friend of mine teaches that friendships should be like a beautiful bouquet of flowers. This is the best analogy that I've ever heard to describe what I feel in my own spirit on this subject. Each friend is to be to a beautiful treasure from the Lord. Each is to be uniquely placed in your life and provide color and fragrance in its own distinctive way.

This is how I see a friendship bouquet in chart form. The left column identifies different roles you play in a variety of friendships. The right column identifies corresponding roles played by those to whom you relate.

FRIENDS YOU RELATE TO

YOUR ROLE AS A FRIEND	THE FRIENDS YOU RELATE TO
The Created Being, the Redeemed, the Saved	The Creator, the Redeemer, the Savior
The Disciple, the Student, the Learner, the Servant	The Guide, the Teacher, the Mentor, the Leader
The Peer Friend	The Peer Friend a. Milestones: You share significant memories together. b. Common Goals: You share common vision, common calling and common purpose. c. Professions: You work at the same location or vocation. d. Intercession: You share burdens and pray together. e. Activities: You have like interests and enjoy doing things together. f. Community: You share small favors and do things for each other in times of need.
The Sister	The Family Friend: Your common bond is your parents. This would be a brother or a sister.
The Daughter	The Parent Friend
The Wife	The Mate, the Spouse
The Mother	The Child Friend
The Discipler, the Mentor	The Disciple, the Student, the New Convert, the Unsaved

You may have other flowers that you would add to this bouquet. However, the point is that friends are all around you. You have but to reach out and embrace them.

A Friend of God

If you are going to be successful as a Christian woman of influence, your very best friend needs to be Jesus Christ. When all other relationships waiver in the wind, this one never will. In Hebrews 13:5, He promises, ". . . I will never leave you nor forsake you." Others may grow weary of your idiosyncrasies, your weaknesses and your strengths, for that matter, but Christ will always be there for you. Psalm 121:3-8 so beautifully says, "He will not allow your foot to be moved; He who keeps you will not slumber. Behold, He who keeps Israel shall neither slumber nor sleep. The Lord is your keeper; the Lord is your shade at your right hand. The sun shall not strike you by day, nor the moon by night. The Lord shall preserve you from all evil; He shall preserve your soul. The Lord shall preserve your going out and your coming in from this time forth, and even forevermore." I call that friendship!

The book of James tells us that Abraham was a "friend of God" (James 2:23). II Chronicles 20:7 and Isaiah 41:8 also refer to Abraham as God's friend. Not only was Abraham God's friend, but God was a friend of his. How did that happen? If there is one friend that would be beneficial to have by your side, certainly that friend is God.

James goes on to tell us that Abraham became God's friend because "he did the works of God," and "he believed God." In other words, he gave his whole person to God. He entrusted his spirit to God by believing Him, and he entrusted his will, mind, emotions and physical labor to God by doing His works. He gave it all! What a pattern!

I think that the biggest aspect to the success of this friendship with God is to realize that He is neither expecting nor desiring some prescribed formula from you. He simply desires your sincere love, communication and obedience.

A Friend to Family Members

If you are a married woman, your husband should be your next best friend. You should laugh together, love together, work together, cry together and pray together. This should be the most endearing friendship you have.

Marriage is not only a covenant made before God, but it is also a covenant of companionship. Evidence of this is found in Malachi 2:13-16, which says, "And this is the second thing you do: you cover the altar of the Lord with tears, with weeping and crying; so He does not regard the offering anymore, nor receive it with good will from your hands. Yet you say, 'For what reason?' Because the Lord has been witness between you and the wife of your youth, with whom you have dealt treacherously; yet she is your companion and your wife by covenant. But did He not make them one, having a remnant of the Spirit? And why one? He seeks godly offspring. Therefore take heed to your spirit, and let none deal treacherously with the wife of his youth. 'For the Lord God of Israel says that He hates divorce, for it covers one's garment with violence,' says the Lord of hosts. 'Therefore take heed to your spirit, that you do not deal treacherously.' " God does not want your husband to deal treacherously with you, nor does He want you to break the covenant of companionship with him.

Mike Mason, in his book, *The Mystery of Marriage*, says it this way: "Marriage is the closest bond that is possible between two human beings. That, at least, was the original idea behind it. . . . As it was originally designed, marriage was a union to end all unions, the very last word, and the first, in human intimacy. Socially, legally, physically, emotionally, every which way, there is just no other means of getting closer to another human being, and never has been, than marriage." Suffice it to say, the best investment you will ever make is in your marriage and in your children. [1]

Many years ago, now, my husband and I decided to work hard at making our children our very closest friends. We are thankful to be able to say that has come to pass. Making your children your friends is one of the most rewarding things that you will ever do. The process requires a definite time commitment, but it is worth every hour that you put into it.

Extended family should be included here, also. If your family members know the Lord, they can be an incredible blessing and strength to you in prayer and many other ways. They know you in ways that no one else will ever know you. In many ways, your extended family members truly are your most intimate friends. They love you with or without your titles, with or without your ability to perform.

1. Mike Mason, <u>The Mystery of Marriage</u>, (Multnomah Publishers, 1985).

If your family members don't know the Lord, continuing to bond and extend love is still the will of God. No one else has a unique blood bond with you like your biological family. God must have a reason for these close relationships.

Whether your family members are geographically close to you or not, they can still be a blessing and a strength to you. My brother and I have lived two thousand miles apart for over twenty-five years, and we rarely see each other. He and his family live geographically near the other members of our biological family, and I do not. When our grandmother died, I went to the funeral without my husband or children. Just as the service was to begin, I was flooded with precious memories of my grandmother, and I began to weep uncontrollably. I stepped out into the hallway at the back of the church, and there was my brother with loving arms to embrace me in my sorrow. Jesus is the ". . . friend who sticks closer than a brother," but the love a brother or sister can offer comforts in ways that no one else can (Proverbs 18:24).

As you and your children or extended family members develop closeness and are in the same church together, you must be careful not to be guilty of nepotism if you are in leadership. Nepotism is putting family members into positions of leadership that they are not called or gifted for, only because of their family ties to you. It is not uncommon for family members to have individual callings, as well as a family calling, upon them. However, you must not place them in ministry positions simply because they are your friends and family members. This can be extremely wounding to others who may have served faithfully and looked forward to having such an opportunity to serve.

On the other hand, neither should you deny family members the opportunity to minister in the capacity that God has called them, simply because you have a fear of criticism. You must release them to minister as you would anyone else in the congregation. If you hinder them from doing so simply because they are family, this also can be wounding to the Body of Christ.

A Friend to Disciples and Mentors

Friendship between a mentor and a student can be very special. You will have some mentors for life, and you will have some only for a season. The same is also true in reverse: you will stay connected in some way with some mentorees for life, and your involvement with some will only be for a season. Do not try to press these relationships into a mold of your own desire. Release your expectations, and let God put the relationships together.

Elijah and Elisha developed a close mentor-disciple relationship. This relationship became so close that even when Elijah told his young student to stay behind, Elisha knew him so well that he refused, knowing that he would not be denied. Elijah told him three times to stay and three times Elisha continued to follow. Finally, after doing a miracle and crossing the Jordan on a dry riverbed, the great mentor turned to the diligent student and said, "Ask! What may I do for you, before I am taken away from you?" Elisha humbly responded, "Please let a double portion of your spirit be upon me" (II Kings 2:9). As Elisha followed the old prophet's command following his request, he watched him closely, and the chariot and horses of fire came and separated them, and a whirlwind took Elijah up into heaven. Elisha saw it all! His eyes were opened to the departure of his mentor. As he watched, he cried out, in verse twelve, "My father, my father . . ."

What had happened to this son of Shaphat? Had he forgotten who his biological father was? No, of course not. He simply had developed a father-son relationship with this mentor and friend, Elijah, so much so that in a moment of separation he called out, "My father, my father . . ." Oh, what tremendous beauty is found in spiritual fathers and mothers and spiritual sons and daughters! What reward, what sweetness to the soul is such friendship!

If you are young, seek out an older woman to mentor you in the ways of the Lord. This is a sign of wisdom, not ignorance. Approach her with a plan but no expectations. In other words, do not require her to become everything that your biological mother has been to you or should have been to you. There are some voids that only Jesus will fill. Psalm 27:10 says, "When my father and my mother forsake me, then the Lord will take care of me."

Don't expect your mentor to fill an emotional void that God has intended to fill Himself. In the course of time this void may be filled, but if you go with the expectation in mind that it will be filled immediately by a specific person, you may be disappointed.

However, approach your would-be mentor with sincere questions and specific desires of what you hope to accomplish through the relationship. Generally speaking, most mentors love sincere, but not intrusive, questions. They enjoy specific goals and hope-filled desires, but not expectations.

When you seek out a mentor, realize that she may not be able to impart to you all that you had hoped for. After all, Elisha got the groceries and washed Elijah's tunics for ten years before he received the double portion mantle. You'll be amazed by what can be imparted to your spirit by working together on projects. Graciously accept what your mentor proffers, and trust God to continue to impart to you personally.

One mentor will not give you everything that you may need. That is God's job. He doesn't want you to become dependent on one person other than Himself. Again, realize that you may have different mentors for various reasons and throughout numerous seasons of your life.

If the person, who you would desire as a mentor, does not feel the same at this time, offer that desire up to the Lord, and release it. Don't allow yourself to become embittered. This is a sharing relationship, and if you don't both agree to it, it won't work. There must be unity in your hearts at the outset for this relationship to work successfully. Maybe this is the right person but the wrong time, or maybe this is the right time but the wrong person.

If you are older, pray for God's direction, and seek out a younger woman to tuck under your wing and instruct in the ways of the Lord. Tell her what you would specifically like to impart to her life, and then leave it up to her to pray and to decide if this is something from which she would like to benefit at this time.

Never push yourself on a younger person. Your age or station may be intimidating to her, and she may say yes without really feeling a link to you from the Lord. It's important that you both feel that this relationship is from the Lord, not just one of you. If she agrees, then lay out your plan, and go for it! Put aside your fear of rejection or your fear of mankind's opinions of your motives, and multiply and increase yourself.

I Corinthians 4:15 says, "For though you might have ten thousand instructors in Christ, yet you do not have many fathers . . ." You do not have to be a certified teacher with multiple degrees to mentor someone. You simply proffer what God has imparted to you personally. When your young disciple reaches a time when she needs to move on, rejoice in the friendship and encourage her to do so. This is like healthy parenting—you raise your children and release them. Please do not stay behind your walls. Young women everywhere today are seeking out mentors.

A Friend to Peers

Whether you are in an official capacity of leadership or not, the area of peer friendships may be a challenge if others see you as a Christian woman of influence. People may evaluate your relationships based on their own desires and definitions, rather than applying God's standards. Although I would like to focus this section on the Christian leader, you may find that, in your place of influence, you can easily relate to these comments as well.

Sometimes peer friendships are actually debated in Christian leadership circles. Some generations of clergy have separated themselves from the laity, and some have not. Some leaders have favored certain people to the point of exclusivity, thereby wounding others, and some have stayed away from any relationships with depth out of fear of being misinterpreted and suffering in loneliness. How sad this is! God must be grieved as He watches leaders turn away from these relationships by which He intends to bless and strengthen them.

Peer friendships should never be exclusive or forbid others access. Exclusivity in any relationship is not healthy. All groups of friends should make it a goal to reach out to others. If they don't, they become introverted and ingrown. Even marriage relationships that do not give out to others in an appropriate manner can become stagnant and ingrown.

As long as your friendship with another doesn't exclude others from entering in or feeling that they can relate to you, don't let the enemy hinder you from reaching out. Even Jesus selected the twelve out of the seventy, and the three out of the twelve, to whom He could relate to more closely. From God's perspective, it is never a problem to have close friends; it only becomes a problem when you don't allow others to enter in as well.

If you're in a position of leadership, you must guard against placing people in positions of leadership simply because they're your friends.

James and John were among Jesus' closest friends. When their mother asked if they could be chosen to sit at His right hand and His left, they probably agreed that they would, indeed, be able to do this. Jesus gave a surprising response to this request. He said, "You will indeed drink My cup, and be baptized with the baptism that I am baptized with; but to sit on My right hand and on My left is not Mine to give, but it is for those for whom it is prepared by My Father" (Matthew 20:23).

Like Jesus, you may have friends who want you to use your influence to place them in strategic or desired positions. Don't do this merely because of your friendship. Your friends will have many opportunities to serve, just as every other member of the Body of Christ is called to serve. Placing them in a position of influence is God's job. When He calls them, He'll place them. Obviously, God may use you, as the instrument to do this, but be sure that you are hearing from Him before doing so. After all, Jesus was diligent to receive direction from the Father before He chose His team of disciples, and He was the Son of God.

On the other hand, you don't want to deny someone a position of leadership simply because he or she is your friend and you're afraid of how it might look to others. If your friend is gifted for the position, it'll be obvious, and you have no need to fear.

Whether in the church or on the job, when you're in a leadership position, it's good for you to have friends who are not in an official leadership position. This helps you to hear the heartbeat of others. Although you must be careful to not take your friend's word as representative of the entire group, you should keep an open ear to him or her.

These friends can also easily lift you out of the constant concerns that weigh you down. Your variety of friends should include some intercessors and some who are just plain fun to be with. Proverbs 17:22 says, "A merry heart does good, like medicine, but a broken spirit dries the bones." Whether they lift you out through intercession or through laughter, every leader needs friends who can help to lift the cares and concerns away, at least for a brief respite.

It's very important that you don't pour out your personal marriage concerns or your knowledge of other people's problems to your peer friends. If you give them knowledge about others that is not for them to know, you may wound others. Gossip is vicious and dangerous.

You do, however, need a friend with whom you can share and relay your concerns. Nevertheless, this friend should be one who is on the same level of leadership, or is in a supervisory position over you. You need someone at this level to whom you can pour your heart out and know that your perspective is understood. You need a friend whom you can trust, one who will not think you should step down from leadership every time you have an emotion out of sorts. Simply said, you need someone with a shared perspective at times.

If you are married, this friend could definitely be your husband. However, because men generally don't think like women, you may sometimes need a female friend who is on the same wavelength and can bear your burden. It should be someone who your husband trusts as well. This person could be a peer or a mentor.

Even at this level, though, you shouldn't share confidences about others, unless you have their permission to do so. People need to know that they can trust you to keep their confidences. If you need another leader's perspective or aid in a situation, simply ask the person for permission. This subject is a whole topic in itself, but suffice it to say, don't gossip about the people to whom you minister or with whom you work.

This kind of friendship should not take away from your relationship with the Lord. Remember Adam in Genesis? God designed us with a need for co-partners. If you do begin to turn to a friend consistently before turning to God, you're setting both you and your friend up for trouble. God doesn't like that, and when God's not happy, nobody's happy. When this begins to happen, you will usually find that your friend begins to avoid contact because your dependence on her has become wearying. Why? Because they're not God.

If you are a leader's wife and don't have any other peer-level friendship opportunities nearby, then seek out another leader's wife. Offer your friendship before you have any major problems or concerns. Offer her your friendship. The Holy Spirit is busy breaking down walls and defenses between people in leadership positions.

Find someone with whom you can take off your garments of praise and just be yourself. Again, of course, this person could be your husband. However, it is certainly appropriate to have other helpful friendships as well. The point is that God has designed a wonderful network of relationships to bless, edify and encourage you. You just need to access them.

How Can I Overcome Hurt and Fear?

Don't say, "I've reached out and been hurt and disappointed before, and I'll not do that again." Perhaps you have had some very hurtful experiences, but God is longing to bless you and heal you through the avenue of forgiveness and trust.

If you are still holding on to a hurt, forgive the one who hurt you and move on. If you've already exercised all of the principles of forgiveness and it still hangs on, then ask someone to pray for you. Ask God to miraculously heal your wounded spirit. Sometimes you just need a miracle. If you do, stop and pray right now that God will release it to you. He loves you. He saw what happened. He was right there. Reach out to Him once again and receive your healing.

If you've been in a spiritual cocoon, hiding from the possibility of hurt, break out of it and fly again. Take one small step at a time and see what the Lord will do. He will gently lead you. Trust Him.

A friend once told me, "Faith says, 'I believe that God can do it for anyone.' Trust says, 'I believe that God will do it for me.'" Trust goes a little deeper, is a little more intimate. Reach out and take the Master's hand. He will do a miracle for you. Psalm 147:3 says, "He heals the brokenhearted and binds up their wounds." If you have a need in this area, reach out and take His healing now—it's yours.

Yes, relationships are risky. Sometimes you'll be disappointed and even hurt. Sometimes you'll be misunderstood and will not be given an opportunity to explain. As much as people try not to expect more out of leaders, they do. They may expect more out of your friendship than they would another, but they may give more to it as well. Don't deny yourself this great opportunity, to be a blessing and to receive a blessing, by assuming the worst. Reach out in faith. As one person told me not long ago, "The best vitamin for gaining friends is B1."

What Else Can I Do to Maintain Healthy Friendships?

At the beginning of this chapter, I told you that this wouldn't be another teaching on friendship as there are many good books out on this subject already. However, I would like to close this chapter with a little checklist for you and your friends to consider when evaluating your relationships.

FRIENDSHIP CHECKLIST

HINDRANCES TO FRIENDSHIP

☐ Self-centeredness: Do I always have to do it my way or at my pace?

☐ Insecurity: Am I able to stand on my own with God? Am I overly dependent on my friend?

☐ Fear: Am I fearful due to past disappointments in other friendships?

☐ Pride: Do I want this person as a friend for prestige?

☐ Expectations: Do I have undisclosed or unrealistic hopes concerning this friendship?

☐ Motives: Do I want this person as a friend for purposes of money or identification?

☐ Backgrounds: Do I understand our cultural, social, religious or family differences?

☐ Geographic Separation: Am I willing to work on this friendship even though we may be separated geographically?

☐ Communication and Social Skills: Am I doing my part in relating?

☐ Words: Are my words negative or positive? (Proverbs 18:21)

☐ Do I gossip with or about my friend? (Proverbs 20:19; 16:28)

☐ Am I sarcastic? (Proverbs 12:18)

☐ Do I give false flattery? (Proverbs 26:28)

☐ Am I dishonest? (Proverbs 6:16-17)

☐ Anger: Am I an angry person? (Proverbs 22:24-25)

☐ Ungodliness: Am I a fool? (I Corinthians 5:11; II Thessalonians 3:14; Psalm 1:1; Proverbs 13:20)

☐ Gluttony: Am I a glutton? Do I lack self-control? (Proverbs 28:7)

☐ Possessiveness

☐ Am I jealous of others intruding on our friendship?

☐ Do I get angry when others want to join us?

☐ Am I exclusive? Do I want this person to be my best and only friend?

☐ Am I emotionally dependent on this friend?

CULTIVATING A HEALTHY FRIENDSHIP

☐ Reach out. (Proverbs 18:24)

☐ Listen. (Proverbs 1:5)

☐ Keep confidences. (Proverbs 11:13; 25:9; 17:9)

☐ Guard your friend's reputation. (Proverbs 17:17; 27:10; I Corinthians 13:6-7)

☐ Communicate directly and honestly. (Proverbs 25:8-10; 27:6, 9; Ephesians 4:15)

☐ Respect your friend's time alone. Limit your visits. (Proverbs 25:17; 27:14)

☐ Share your friend's joys and concerns. (Romans 12:15)

☐ Give of yourself unselfishly. (Philippians 2:3-4; John 15:12-13; I John 3:16)

☐ Forgive when necessary. (Matthew 18:21; I Corinthians 13:5)

THE "ONE ANOTHER" CHALLENGE

Love one another . . . . John 13:34; I John 3:18

Comfort one another . . . . .I Thessalonians 4:18

Consider one another . . . . .Hebrews 10:24

Exhort one another . . . . .Hebrews 3:13

Edify one another . . . . .Romans 14:19

Admonish one another . . . . .Romans 15:14

Minister to one another . . . . .I Peter 4:10

Forbear one another . . . . .Colossians 3:13

Submit to one another . . . . .Ephesians 5:21

Forgive one another . . . . .Ephesians 4:32

Teach one another . . . . .Colossians 3:16

Prefer one another . . . . .Romans 12:10; 13:7

Pray for one another . . . . .James 5:16

Be hospitable to one another . . . . .I Peter 4:9

Greet one another . . . . .I Peter 5:14

Fellowship with one another . . . . .I John 1:7

Eat with one another . . . . .Acts 2:46

Think with one another . . . . .Philippians 2:2

Share material possessions with one another . . . . .Acts 2:45

Embrace one another . . . . .I Corinthians 16:20

Bear one another's burdens . . . . .I Corinthians 12:26;
Galatians 6:2

Rejoice with one another . . . . .I Corinthians 12:26

Restore one another . . . . .Galatians 6:1

Work with one another . . . . .Colossians 4:11;
Hebrews 10:24

Worship with one another .Hebrews 10:25

Chapter 12

MARRIAGE
A Woman of Covenant Commitment

My husband and I recently ministered at a Valentine's weekend conference. During the conference, a delegated couple would sing a love song to each other before each teaching session began.

One couple, who had been married for over thirty-five years, stood holding hands, looking into each other's eyes, and the husband began to sing to his wife, "You are my Valentine." This was a new song that he had written for her for this occasion. It was especially touching and meaningful because they had been married for such a significant amount of time.

As the husband sang to his wife, "You're not just my dream. You're my dream come true," she looked endearingly at him. Not one love-emotion was left untouched in the room. Husbands and wives alike were obviously being softened in the atmosphere of love. My husband and I agreed that this was the purest, momentary display of human love and adoration that we had ever publicly observed. It was precious and saturated with sincere love.

I asked the wife, later, how she could stand, looking into her husband's eyes as he sang this tender and adoring song to her, without crumbling emotionally. (I would have melted into the floor, I think.) Her response, with a sweet smile on her face, was, "He's been writing songs for me since I was twelve years old." I stood in amazement, not only at the precious musical gift, but also at the pure and deep godly love each had for the other.

Your husband may not be able to write beautiful songs or poetry. He may even struggle to articulate or demonstrate his feelings for you. However, if he is a man with whom you have made a covenant before God, then he is your treasure.

What Type of Wife Am I?

There are probably three categories of wives reading this chapter: one painfully hurting, one contentedly happy and one enthusiastically rejoicing in the goodness of her husband. The love in your marriage may be so rich and full that you almost have a hard time believing that any Christian marriage could have problems. If this is not the case, your marriage may be so needy that you are already trying to decide whether to do away with it. Somewhere in between are the many who go back and forth but keep working on it.

Enthusiastically Rejoicing

If you are enthusiastically rejoicing, keep rejoicing. Don't hesitate to share how good it is when two walk together in sacrificial love toward one another. The message needs to get out!

However, share in humility, and honestly confess that the key is hard work and complete dependence on the Lord. Be watchful, and remain ever humble. Humility and watchfulness will keep mercy and grace at your doorstep. ". . . God resists the proud, but gives grace to the humble" (James 4:6).

Pray and ask the Lord to give you increasing discernment and compassion for those who hide behind closed doors of secret abuse. They hide under the strong hand of misdefined grace, arrogance and legalistic holiness.

Painfully Hurting

If you are painfully hurting, the heart of the Lord Jesus is extended to you today, as it was on the day the offense(s) occurred. Feel free to let your defenses down, come into a quiet place and receive healing from the Master Covenant-Maker. He loves you.

Not only will He right the wrongs, but He will also remove the sting of the wound that has been inflicted. If you have let your sword of trust fall by your side, raise it once again and take a brave step.

Somewhere in Between

If you are somewhere in between, keep faithfully working on this wonderful gift of marriage. It's worth every moment that you invest. I pray that this chapter will add insight to your understanding and will increase your faith to believe for more good days than bad days, more prosperous years than lean years. Continue to send the hurtful issues down the avenue of forgiveness, and work hard at building happy memories together. Most of all, keep your sense of humor in tact. This journey will include a little of the unexpected, just to build your faith.

What Is the True Meaning of Covenant?

In the midst of the joy and the pain is covenant, the covenant that you and your husband made together before God. When a marriage partner breaks promises that were made on the wedding day, he or she sins against the marriage. The sin is not just against oneself, but against his or her spouse, because the two became one when they made covenant before God. When you and your husband made covenant with one another, you became partakers of one another's lives, for better or for worse. If one of you succeeds, both of you succeed. If one of you falls, both of you are affected. That is the power of covenant.

Don't misunderstand. We each must account for our own individual sins before God. You cannot pay for your spouse's sins, nor can he pay for yours since in reality Jesus paid for them already. However, you are affected by one another's sin because you are bound together in covenant, and you walk down the pathway of pain and healing together.

Covenant-making is the basis of our salvation in Christ Jesus. Throughout history God has always been a covenant-making God. Marriage is a covenant commitment modeled after God's covenants. My husband, Ken, charts the parallels between marriage and God's covenants this way.

COVENANTS

GOD'S COVENANTS	THE MARRIAGE COVENANT
Promises made	Vows made
Ratification by blood	Life and death commitment
Seal or token	Rings given
Sanctuary or altar	Church or altar
Feast of celebration	Reception or feast of celebration
Name given	Name given

As you can see, everything about the way a typical wedding ceremony is performed is based on covenant.

Even the body of a woman is created in such a way as to reflect covenant reality. Medical doctors say that there is no evident purpose for the hymen in a woman's body. The hymen is a thin mucous membrane that exists at the opening of the vagina before it's broken. It can be broken in a variety of ways prior to sexual intercourse. However, sexual intercourse cannot occur without breaking it. When it's broken, there is a slight shedding of blood. Perhaps this is a sign of the ratification of the covenant.

(For more study of God's covenants, I would recommend *The Covenants* by Kevin J. Conner and Ken Malmin, City Bible Publishing.)

What Pressures Can Challenge Christian Marriages?

It is a privilege to walk together and serve together. As I mentioned in the first chapter, I believe it is the will of God for every woman to function uniquely according to her individual calling. However, there are certain challenges that every Christian wife faces as she determines to be a positive influence on the world around her. This will happen whether she feels called or not, whether she says much or says little and whether she wants the responsibility of being a visible Christian or not. There is no way around it. People will have certain expectations, not because of who she is, but because of the One whom her marriage is meant to reflect.

You can either accept or reject the challenge of being an example. Even if you try to tell people that you don't consider your marriage to be an example of a good Christian marriage they will still watch you. You can't stop this from happening. Married people everywhere are looking for role models who make marriage work, and they expect Christians to know how to make it work, whether they really do or not. The pressure to be an example of a Christian marriage can be intimidating. Though the help of the Lord is faithful, the pressure can be intense.

Every vocation has its unique pressures as well. Whether one or both of you work(s) at a labor-intensive job, a people-skills job or a corporate level job, each has its unique challenges. Each places its own unique demands on the marriage. Christian marriages are certainly not exempt from these pressures.

Every minister's wife has her moments of stretching, just like every Christian wife. It is said that Billy Graham's wife, Ruth, was once asked, "Would you ever consider divorce?" Her response was, "Divorce, no. Murder, yes." This well-known evangelist's wife was only joking when she said this. However, her response does demonstrate that frustration comes knocking on everyone's door from time to time.

If your husband is doing his best to serve the Lord, don't complain, but rejoice that you're married to such a man, and determine to walk together regardless of the circumstances. If you continue to focus on the sacrifices, you will set yourself up as a martyr. (By the way, consider the fact that martyrs are not really martyrs until they are dead! There is so much life to enjoy between now and then!) People with a victim mentality certainly do not inspire others to follow in their footsteps. Why not rejoice instead of complaining?

What Is Required of Me As the Wife of a Leader?

Regardless of the extent of your valued input and active involvement in the church, what most leaders want is a wife who gives responsive love, is happy, knows how to hear from God herself, and will follow his lead. Additionally, although some husbands may be hesitant to mention it openly in these contemporary times, most still really like nutritious meals and well-kept homes. How's that for a convicting little checklist?

In the next few pages, I would like to address some specific issues for women who are married to men in key areas of Christian leadership. Whether you and your husband are lay leaders or church staff leaders, some unique pressures will come to bear on your marriage. While I am discussing these issues primarily from the standpoint of ministerial leadership, many of the same principles will also apply to women whose husbands hold positions of leadership in the community or on the job.

The Realities of Leadership

The following list describes how a wife might need to respond to her husband based on the attributes of his leadership role.

REALITIES OF LEADERSHIP

WORK OF THE MINISTRY	MINISTER NEEDS HIS WIFE TO
PRESSURE TRAITS OF THE MINISTRY:	
1. Performance oriented.	1. Let him be himself so he does not have to perform at home.
2. Making judgement calls (he must be right).	2. Give him room to fail. Offer forgiveness.
3. Serious.	3. Be joyful. Let laughter fill the home.
4. Sometimes tedious (paperwork, etc.).	4. Be exciting.
5. Pressure-packed.	5. Be a place of refuge in her heart and in her home.
6. Hearing constant verbiage.	6. Be quiet, in word at times, in spirit always.
7. Dealing with sin.	7. Be an unselfish, giving lover.
8. Facing people with facades.	8. Be real, transparent and honest.
9. Busy and hectic.	9. Be peaceful.
10. Demanding.	10. Be giving.
11. Lonely.	11. Be with him spirit, soul and body.
12. Discouraging.	12. Be encouraging.
INCENTIVE TRAITS OF THE MINISTRY:	
1. Fulfilling.	1. Be affectionate, intimate and fulfilling.
2. Challenging.	2. Be flexible and excited with challenge.
3. Contemporary and current.	3. Be current in her thinking and willing to learn.
4. Hearing the Lord.	4. Hear and respond to the Lord.
5. Knowing the Word of God.	5. Be knowledgeable of the Word of God.
6. Relating to varieties of people.	6. Be willing to relate to varieties of people.
7. Active.	7. Be active, not lazy.
8. In order (his office, his staff, etc.).	8. Have her children and her home in order.
9. Loving people and being loved by people.	9. Be loving, thoughtful and kind.
10. Authority.	10. Be submissive to his leadership in the home.
11. Having sincere relationships with others.	11. Be willing to develop sincere friendships.
12. Placement and travel.	12. Be willing to be in God's will regardless of the geographic placement.

This list looks a bit overwhelming, doesn't it? Obviously, I haven't touched on all that you need your husband to be, but then that would be another book. This one is for you.

Essentially, your husband needs to focus on the ways that Christ can meet his needs, and not on what you do for him. However, you need to be aware of the real issues of his subconscious desires. Although he may have been hesitant to mention them before, you now have an opportunity to objectively discuss them together.

Don't allow this list to pressure you. Simply let it motivate you in your attitudes and actions toward your husband. Talk to him about it. He may have an entirely different list than this, or his may only partially relate to this one. Use this list as a tool to open up a heartfelt discussion with your husband. When you do this, be sure to leave your ego outside on the doorstep. Be grateful for the accolades, and take the challenges to heart.

The Attraction of a Man In Leadership

Have you ever asked yourself, "How do the mighty fall? And how can our marriage stand?" To answer these questions, you really need to understand the realities of ministry from the male perspective and what makes a Christian leader more attractive to women than the average man.

Men in ministry, as men in other professional and public fields, have a certain magnetic attraction. Generally speaking, this attraction is stronger than that of a man in a less causative vocation. Women sometimes have a difficult time recognizing the humanity through the veil of position.

As the wife of a minister, business leader, athletic coach or teacher, you may not always see this attractiveness because you live with the reality of the leadership calling and the man himself. Others, however, don't live with your reality, and they may think they would like your reality better than theirs.

My goal is not to frighten you or make you suspicious of other women. However, I do want you to realize that even if your husband is sloppy, arrogant and unkind, he may still be a temptation to another woman simply because of his Christian leadership position.

There are four basic things that attract a woman to a man: self-confidence, power, public recognition and a demonstrated interest and concern toward others. I realize that other spiritual qualities could be added to this brief list, but these are the most basic elements of attraction for both Christian and non-Christian women.

In looking at these four areas, notice how the role of a Christian leader exemplifies all of them. No Christian leader is entirely self-confident, but he definitely walks in confidence and assurance in the knowledge of the Lord. He purports vision and future direction for people to follow. He exudes confidence. He also has power that has been given to him by the ordination of the Lord, especially if he is in a sacred position of authority in the church. If so, he is a spiritual covering, responsible for many before the Lord. The Christian leader also receives public recognition and praise from others. While he may have critics, he still receives esteem and honor from the people he serves. Part of a pastor's calling is to shepherd the flock with care and concern. He not only preaches, but he prays and counsels with people. He visits the sick and shows compassion to the hurting. A Christian athletic coach or business leader similarly demonstrates wisdom and compassion for those directly under his care.

All of the qualities that open the heart of a woman to intimacy are qualities that God ordained to define the calling of a pastor or Christian leader. God did not arrange this correspondence, of course, so people would fall morally. He plainly desires that a leader be a man after His own heart and likeness.

As a leader's wife, you should protect the vulnerabilities that go with these God-given advantages. Though your husband needs to be revered to fulfill his mission, he also needs to be protected from those who may misunderstand their attraction.

While others may believe your husband to be a man of perfection, you will become well aware of his imperfections. Author and speaker, Lee Ezell, speaks of a husband's humanness with this illustration. She says, "You thought you married Prince Charming, but then you found out that he had a horse to clean up after."

Not all, but most women have had, at some time, a desire to marry someone as nearly perfect as possible. Many pray about it, counsel with others and even fast before making the decision to marry. They get married with confidence in their choice and soon discover that there is this illusive horse to clean up after. It could not be the "prince" who leaves his coat on the kitchen chair, the milk out on the counter or the dirty laundry on the floor next to the waiting hamper. No, the "prince" wouldn't do such things. It must be someone else in the house. (The problem is that this all usually happens long before children arrive or are old enough to crawl around and take the blame for these things.)

Yes, you live with the prince who so many admire with rare hesitation. (You admired him, as well, when his mother was covering his tracks.) Yet his perfection eludes you as you work hard, keep the home in order, make sure his laundry is current and stand by his side ever faithfully.

What I am trying to communicate, humorously, is actually a sad reality. Many Christian leaders' wives struggle with receiving from their husbands, personally and ministerially, when they are inconsiderate at home. When this happens consistently, husbands and wives must talk about it and come to some workable solutions. If they don't, they will experience downward spirals in their marriages.

Even though you see the humanity of your husband, even the frailty and weaknesses, you must work at loving him as you desire to be loved. If you don't, there may be another woman who will. Be well aware of these issues, and guard your marriage. Yes, your husband is human, but so are you.

Let's return now to the realities faced in all Christian marriages.

How Can I Recognize a Downward Spiral in My Marriage?

Within the marriage roles, every husband and wife has some basic needs. Of course, these needs are to be met primarily in Christ. However, it is easier for each spouse to respond if each is doing his or her best to sacrificially love and serve the other.

A husband's most basic need is to receive respect and intimacy from his wife. A wife, on the other hand, desires provision and cherishing from her husband. When these needs are not fulfilled, a digression begins. It may happen something like this.

A wife desires adequate provision and meaningful cherishing.

Her expectations are disappointed. She sees that her prince has feet of clay.

She loses respect for him.

She becomes ungrateful. She begins to resist his decisions and wants to make decisions on her own.

Intimacy breaks down. She begins to resist his physical affection. This becomes an unspoken crushing to his spirit.

His estimation of himself is wounded. He is confused by what is happening but is afraid to ask for fear that he may not be able to measure up to her desire.

He attempts to improve matters. He attempts to ignore the fact that there is an obvious problem, pretends that there is no problem, or attempts to correct the problem with gifts and evenings out. He fears actually discussing what the real problem may be, so his prayers remain hindered because the unity is broken between them.

She builds resentment. She does not understand his fear, and though she may initially respond to the gifts, inwardly she becomes angry and resentful.

She tires of his vision or lack of vision. She becomes lackadaisical and just does not care anymore about his vision or desires. Or, she inwardly becomes ambivalent and feels trapped.

He buries himself in more vocational busyness, gives up on his ministry or loses hope for his marriage. He becomes a workaholic, quits or becomes tempted to seek out another for intimacy and falls morally.

This digression illustrates what can happen when a wife experiences a lack of provision or cherishing. It also demonstrates what a husband experiences when there is a lack of responsive love from his wife. It is a hurtful and unnecessary digression, but it happens more commonly than Christians like to acknowledge. If you will give yourself to transparency and sacrificial love for your husband, you can stop this digression at any point you feel it has begun to take place.

What Are Some Hindrances to Oneness in Marriage?

In John 10:10 Jesus warns, "The thief does not come except to steal, and to kill, and to destroy. I have come that they may have life, and that they may have it more abundantly." Satan's ploy is to rob and steal from you and from your marriage. Sometimes he will even use things that appear to be good to steal from you. In fact, it usually is the pursuit of the "good" that distracts from the pursuit of the "best." Sometimes, the hindrance will not be a direct attack of Satan, but simply your own thoughtlessness.

If there was ever something worth investing your heart and mind in, it's your marriage. To invest in your marriage is to invest in the power to influence others for Christ. To steal from your marriage is to hurt the effectiveness of your influence as a Christian.

Let's look at some of the common hindrances to developing oneness in marriage.

Having Too Many Individualized Activities

Going in opposite directions too many days and evenings of the week can take its toll. While business associations, community involvement and church are important, if your schedule is full with individual activities, your marriage relationship will suffer for lack of time together.

Not Scheduling Time for Togetherness

If you don't schedule time together, you probably won't find many windows of time to spend together. There will always be one more person to encourage or one more communique to get in the mail.

Not Communicating Regularly or Meaningfully

Marriage combines two busy schedules, the concerns of the family and active involvement in the church, to produce a relationship that is challenged by the many directional pulls of active life. You must continually work at communicating in order to maintain a close bond in the midst of the busyness.

Not Resolving Differences That Arise

Intimacy is easier to destroy than it is to build. Ignoring or pretending that differences don't happen doesn't resolve them. Give yourself time to grow together in oneness. Let the "two become one." Don't expect your husband to be as good at intimacy as social commentators may demand him to be.

Communicating in a Hurtful Way

Ask yourself, "Do my words invite my spouse into my heart, or do they push him away?" If your words have not been full of grace lately, repent to the Lord and to your husband. Never attack your spouse. Always attack the issue that is at the root of the problem. If you do attack him, be quick to ask for forgiveness.

Being Dishonest

Deception never helps; it hinders transparency.

Nagging

If your husband wanted another parent, he would not have gotten married. Once you have plainly said something to him and you know it's been heard, drop it with your husband and take it to the Lord.

Behaving Abusively or Violently

Abusive behavior is damaging to the spirit and soul, as well as to the body. The repercussions of abuse will also wound those around you. Get counsel and prayer from a trusted leader if this is plaguing your marriage.

Being Unfaithful

There is nothing that wounds a marriage more than emotional or literal infidelity. It extracts from the covenant stone on which a marriage is built. It places the marriage under the judgement of God rather than the blessing of God. It exchanges insecurity for trust, pain for joy and rejection for love. The moment emotional infidelity becomes a seed in your heart, root it out and toss it into the darkest sea. Yielding to the temporary illusion of excitement will never be worth the agony you will reap. Forgiveness, healing and reconciliation can come, but the process can be scarring not only to yourself, but to many standing nearby and many more who are looking on.

How Can I Build a Marriage That Lasts?

Intergrate, Don't Isolate

Proverbs 14:1 says, "The wise woman builds her house, but the foolish pulls it down with her hands." Although your husband is responsible before God to be the head of the home, you also have a divine responsibility to be a co-laborer and builder of the house.

The greatest key that my husband and I have discovered to make a busy marriage successful is to integrate attitudes, schedules and activities. Don't separate your marriage from your vocation or calling. Let the two complement each other, rather than becoming enemies of each other. If you don't do this, the church or the office can become like another other woman in your marriage.

Of course, you'll have times of intimate sharing when you may take the phone off the hook, lock the door and not invite others to come in. However, these times will be more easily respected if family members and friends feel that you genuinely rejoice in their part in your lives and are not just anxious to get away from them.

Release Your Expectations to God

Loosely hold your husband in the palm of your hand. Let him go. Let him find himself and get established in his place of ministry or vocation. This is crucial to your marriage and your calling together.

After my husband and I had been married a few years and our children were very young, the Lord began to open up opportunities for him to travel and minister abroad as well as at home. As much as I adored our children and was excited that my husband had these opportunities, the diapers piled up and the days passed by, and I began to feel a bit left out.

One day, during my devotional time with the Lord, He began to deal with me. He showed me a picture of myself, holding my husband in the palm of my hand with a tight grip. Then, revealing the pain of the dilemma in my heart, He showed me His hand prying off mine. He gently reminded me that my husband belonged to Him long before he belonged to me.

That day a dam from within broke, and tears of relinquishment flowed like a newly released river. After praying and repenting, I wrote a note of release to my husband and gave it to him that afternoon. That evening he went to church and led the worship service. Afterward a friend came up to him and said, "What has happened to you? You have been released!"

My husband hadn't felt that I had held him back in any way. He assumed that this note of release was more my issue with the Lord than an issue between the two of us. However, after this comment, he did wonder what was going on from God's perspective.

If you have been emotionally holding your husband back from being fully released to minister in the capacity that he is called to, release him. Seek the Lord, ask Him why you are hesitant and deal with the issues. If your struggle is between yourself and the Lord, work on it. If there are issues between yourself and your husband, talk openly and transparently with him about it. For the sake of the purposes of Christ in both of your lives, release.

Do Not Compare

In releasing your husband to respond fully to the Lord, be sure to let him be who God has called him to be. Don't expect him to be someone other than who he is. Don't compare his gifts and talents with someone else's or look longingly at another man's ability to function, coveting that same ability for your husband. II Corinthians 10:12 says, ". . . But they, measuring themselves by themselves, and comparing themselves among themselves, are not wise." Comparison destroys relationships. Your husband will never be fully released if he feels that you're disappointed in him vocationally or personally.

If the place or manner, in which your husband functions, is an embarrassment or struggle for you, ask yourself why it is. Is it because of pride that you want him to function differently, or is it a sincere desire to see him fulfill his potential? Are you looking at his potential or your own ego? Are you measuring fruit by your own standards or by the Lord's?

Your husband will need your encouragement to expand and increase in his ministry and vocational development. However, if that encouragement isn't pure, he will resist it. Comparison will not only affect your husband, but it may also affect your children and those close to you. People can sense when appropriate admiration is lacking in a marriage.

Be the one person in his life who consistently builds him up as a person, a believer, a brother, a man, a friend, a husband and a man of God. Determine to make him a success out of a pure motivation to see his life bring honor to the Lord.

Be Submissive

I once heard a story about Queen Victoria and Prince Albert of England. As the story goes, they got into a disagreement with each other and Prince Albert stormed off to his chambers. The queen came to his door and demanded to be allowed entrance. There was no response from the other side of the door. Once again, the queen knocked loudly and proclaimed, "It's the queen of England. I demand that you let me in!" Again came no response from the other side of the door. Next, the queen knocked ever so slightly and sweetly said, "Albert, it's me, Victoria. May

I please come in?" At this petition, the door was opened. No man wants to be ordered around by his wife, even if she is a queen. He may endure it, but somewhere between the order and the enduring, there is lost love. Ephesians 5:22-24 clearly states, "Wives, submit to your own husbands, as to the Lord. For the husband is head of the wife, as also Christ is head of the church; and He is the Savior of the body. Therefore, just as the church is subject to Christ, so let the wives be to their own husbands in everything."

Whether one is a wife in the twenty-first century or in a period of early church history, the biblical instruction remains the same. Whether one is a wife of a poor man or a rich man, an unregenerate or a pastor, the biblical instruction remains the same on this issue. Wives are to submit to their husbands.

Submission does not mean stifling all perspectives and gifts. God has given those to you to use. Godly submission requires that you give your perspective and release your gifts, or you are not truly acting in submission at all. A lack of involvement is mere subservience, and that's not submission. While it may require patience and timing, sharing your perspectives and talents is part of your calling. Submission is very active. It's a voluntary attitude of the heart. It's an attitude of faith that says, "I trust you." Give it as a gift to your husband.

Be Loyal

Proverbs 31:11-12, which I referred to in the fifth chapter, says of the virtuous woman, "The heart of her husband safely trusts her; so he will have no lack of gain. She does him good and not evil all the days of her life."

Proverbs 4:23 says, "Keep your heart with all diligence . . ." You will not succeed as a trustworthy wife and co-laborer if you don't keep your heart. If you find that you are in a season of struggle and your thoughts are wandering, you may want to consider a fast. There is nothing quite like fasting to convince your soul that your spirit is in charge.

Don't be a complainer. As a Christian, you are called to be a woman of loyalty and faith. If you complain about your furniture or financial inability to go out for dinner, you belittle your husband's ability to provide, and this brings reproach to the testimony of the Lord's faithfulness. Don't complain, rather pray and trust.

Never belittle your husband to others, privately or in front of him. That is disloyalty! If you feel that he needs some adjustment, speak to him privately. If he will not adjust, then seek to understand why, and take it to the Lord. But never belittle him. Only say the kinds of things about your husband that you would like said about you. Only speak of him in the same manner that you would like him to speak of you. When you both have faith that this is what you each can count on from the other, trust is enshrouded in safety, and a lasting house is being built.

Cherish the Intimacy in Your Relationship

Love is not just spoken; it is demonstrated. The demonstration of your love could include cooking, cleaning, praying for him and encouraging him, but it also means enjoying your sexual relationship with him. Titus 2:4 says that the older women are to teach the younger women ". . . to love their husbands . . ." To paraphrase this a bit, you need to be a "husband lover."

The most important thing that I could say about your sexual relationship with your husband is that it is sacred and it is private between the two of you and the Lord. For the most part, your life should be an open book before the people whom you are called to influence for Christ. However, your sexual relationship is not a part of the knowledge to which they should have access. Privacy honors the sacredness of the sexual union and guards its meaningfulness.

The details of this aspect of your marriage should not be available to your friends, family or any others. You will find that your husband will be more motivated to be more creative in lovemaking if he's confident that it's private between the two of you. If he suspects that you are sharing it with others, his creativity will be stifled. If you are unsure about the importance of this, ask him today how important sexual privacy is to him.

Of course, if there is abuse in this area, seek counsel from an older woman (Titus 2:4) of God. By "private" I don't mean hiding pain, confusion or perversion.

In Song of Solomon 4:12-15, the young husband proclaimed of his bride, "A garden enclosed is my sister, my spouse, a spring shut up, a fountain sealed. . . . A fountain of gardens, a well of living waters, and streams from Lebanon." In the deserts of Israel, it was common to place walls around gardens to protect them from the desert winds. The bride-groom was complimenting the beauty of his bride. The only evident problem was that he could not get into the garden to enjoy the pleasures that were prepared for him there. The garden was totally enclosed.

In verse sixteen, the bride cried out, "Awake, O north wind, and come, O south! Blow upon my garden, that its spices may flow out. Let my beloved come to his garden and eat its pleasant fruits." When she realized that he was unable to get into the garden, she called upon the winds to come to her aid.

There may be times when you should rest from everything and everyone, and your husband will need to be sensitive to your needs as well. Love doesn't push itself on another person.

However, there will be other times when, due to a variety of rea-sons, your walls may be up. They won't just protect you from one more wearying intrusion, but may actually hinder your husband from coming in. He may call out to you that he longs to be near, but you may feel too weary to respond. That is when you must call out to the Lord and request that His Spirit blow afresh on you and refresh your soul, that you may enjoy love with your husband once again. Sometimes it may be helpful just to visualize yourself laying all of the cares of your day outside the bedroom door. Your worries are still there to be tended to, but they are on hold.

In actuality, your brain is the primary organ in your body that controls your sexual responses. Your body will usually behave as your brain dictates. When your mind is not working due to stress overload, call out to the Lord, and ask for help. Your destiny is to be a "husband lover," not a "husband rejecter."

According to I Corinthians 7:2-5, you have a divine privilege and responsibility to be available to your husband sexually, except for mutually agreed upon times of fasting and prayer. This passage reads, "Nevertheless, because of sexual immorality, let each man have his own wife, and let each woman have her own husband. Let the husband render to his wife the affection due her, and likewise also the wife to her husband. The wife does not have authority over her own body, but the husband does. And likewise the husband does not have authority over his own body, but the wife does. Do not deprive one another except with consent for a time, that you may give yourselves to fasting and prayer; and come together again so that Satan does not tempt you because of your lack of self-control."

In other words, do not take your husband for granted. Just because he's a godly man doesn't mean that he doesn't desire an intimate, enjoyable sexual relationship with you. If he had wanted to be celibate, he probably would have chosen that lifestyle.

One of the keys to succeeding at this availability is not to allow yourself to pour out the entirety of your energy during the day to other people and causes. This will not always be possible, of course. But as far as a pattern goes, make it your goal to always have some emotional and physical energy reserved to give to your mate. Think about him during the day, and delight in those thoughts. If you have the emotional and physical energy, the sexual desire will not be a problem.

Be sure that you know your husband intimately. Be sensitive to his needs. The closer you grow in your friendship, the more sensitive you'll be to his desires. Help to lift the load by being a fun and affectionate person. We all have a tendency to love others in the way that we would want to be loved. Likely, your husband's definition of affection is different than yours, so work hard at ministering to him in ways that he would desire, though they may not necessarily be the same ways that you would desire. Learn what he likes, and respond accordingly.

Be Spiritually Responsive

Learn how to draw out your husband's spiritual potential in the home as well as at church. If you are not pleased with his personal walk with the Lord, don't pressure him about it. Pressure stifles spiritual motivation.

Pray for him, and concentrate on meeting his other basic needs. If he has to be constantly running to the store to get groceries, is embarrassed to bring a friend by the house because it's in disarray, or never knows if he is going to have a clean shirt to wear, he doesn't have time to pray. If you take care of all the basics and he still fills up the time with other things, then the issue is between him and the Lord. No amount of nagging or pressure will help. Just stay out of the way, so the Lord can deal with him.

On the other hand, if your husband is trying to lead the family devotionally in the Word and prayer, have a positive attitude. Be willing to do whatever part he asks you to do.

If your husband ministers a word publicly, don't correct or adjust it immediately following the service. If you feel that it needs some adjustment for future reference, then wait for the right time, and do it ever so tactfully. Think of how you might like to receive correction if you were the one being adjusted.

Allow your husband times away from the family to fast, pray and wait on God at least once or twice a year. These times will encourage him and give him fresh direction for the family and for other important areas of your life together. God might even tell him something that you have been trying to tell him for months!

What Else Can I Do to Make My Marriage Fulfilling?

Being a Christian wife is certainly not the easiest job in the world, but it can be one of the most fulfilling. After all, Jesus is on your side. He has called you and will anoint you to walk in it. In summary, be sure that you know how to reach God in prayer. Every marriage needs to be under the canopy of prayer.

Be a serious co-partner when things in life are serious, and laugh and have fun when they are not. Cherish your moments with your husband. Stir his love toward you and toward the Lord everyday. If you do, someday he might just sing, "You're not just my dream. You're my dream come true."

What follows are just a couple of assignments that I have added for your enjoyment and, perhaps, for your stretching.

Reaffirmation Vows

"I _____, reaffirm my vow to you, _____, as my wedded wife. I promise to love and cherish you, using as my example the love that Christ has for the church. I promise to provide for your material needs, to be to you a source of strength, to offer you understanding and companionship, joy and peace. I promise to encourage and release you in the gifts the Lord has given to you for the sake of His Body, to offer you leadership and inspiration, to remain forever near. I promise to offer you tenderness and not deprive you of our sexual relationship except during agreed upon times of seeking the Lord. I promise to be loyal and faithful to you, denying all others access to our marriage bed. For better or for worse, in sickness or in health, in riches or in poverty, according to God's holy covenant, I give myself only and always to you until death itself parts us."

"I _____, reaffirm my vow to you, _____, as my wedded husband. I promise to love, honor and respect you, and to be submissive to you as to the Lord. I promise to be a helper fitting to you and your calling, to provide that which is necessary for your well-being, comfort and happiness. I promise to encourage and release you in the gifts that the Lord has given to you for the sake of His Body, to offer you companionship and inspiration, to remain forever by your side. I promise to offer you responsive tenderness and not deprive you of our sexual relationship except during agreed upon times of seeking the Lord. I promise to be loyal and faithful to you, denying all others access to our marriage bed. For better or for worse, in sickness or in health, in riches or in poverty, according to God's holy covenant, I give myself only and always to you until death itself parts us."

Your "Desire List" for Romance

Men and woman often have different preferences in areas of romance. Please use this assignment as an exercise to communicate those preferences with your spouse. Have your husband make his own list as well and discuss them. Where there are differences, try to arrive at acceptable compromises or alternate ideas. Circle or describe all of your special preferences. Add others too.

SETTING: Moonlit beach, Fireplace, Favorite room, Favorite Restaurant? Describe other favorite settings.

MUSIC: What types of music, specific songs or artists?

LIGHTING: Bright, Dim, Candles, Sunset, Sunrise? Describe other conditions.

OTHER HELPS: Favorite Fragrances, Favorite Meals? Describe other preferences.

Redo this assignment every few years. Remember that desires can change in different seasons of life.

Chapter 13

CHILDREN
A Mother Who Imparts Her Anointing

Whether you are a married or single mother, your children are your most valuable asset, your greatest responsibility and your most important ministry. They are your fruit that remains. They will extend your life here on earth, even beyond death, as they carry an impartation of you and the Christ in you to your grandchildren and following generations.

How Does the Lord Feel About Children?

Psalm 127:3-5 says, "Behold, children are a heritage from the Lord, the fruit of the womb is a reward. Like arrows in the hand of a warrior, so are the children of one's youth. Happy is the man who has his quiver full of them; they shall not be ashamed, but shall speak with their enemies in the gate."

I Timothy 3:12-13 says, "Let deacons be the husbands of one wife, ruling their children and their own houses well. For those who have served well as deacons obtain for themselves a good standing and great boldness in the faith which is in Christ Jesus."

Titus 1:6 says, "The elders should be men who are of unquestionable integrity and are irreproachable, the husband of one wife whose children are well trained and are believers not open to accusation of being loose in morals and conduct or unruly and disorderly" (Amplified).

As you can see from these scriptures, children are very important to God. He considers them to be so important that He not only speaks of them and to them in Scripture, but He also gives specific instruction to Christian leaders in regard to how they handle their own children. Any Christian mother who desires to significantly influence others for Christ, must do her best to serve, train and influence in a godly fashion the children God has given her.

As Jesus walked the earth, He made a point to give attention and affection to children. He blessed them, welcomed them and used them as illustrations to teach lessons to his disciples and others around him. God places an obvious premium on children.

Just as He considers the covenant of marriage to be important, He also considers parenting to be important. In the Psalm 127 passage, He says that they are your ". . . heritage from the Lord. . ." This word "heritage" means that they are your priceless heirlooms, treasures whose seed has been passed down from generation to generation. They are the precious seed that originates in Christ.

As we have noted, God so values children that He stresses the importance of the parent-child relationship by insisting that church leaders' families be examples to the congregation. He knows that if leaders place a premium on their children, others will be motivated to follow that example. He also knows that if leaders don't do this, others may follow that negative example.

I know of no greater pressure or challenge on Christian parents today than to accomplish the task of raising godly children. I also know of no greater joy or sense of fulfillment in Christian parents than when they see the obvious fruit of a job well done. Other than God Himself, no one else has more power to humble or exalt you than your children do.

As a young leader, I was very fortunate to have as an example a senior pastor's wife who held her family in high esteem. By loving them everyday in very tangible ways, she made incredible personal sacrifices to see that her children grew up to love God and His house. As she did this, she was to them a beautiful example of Christ and the joy of the calling to serve Him. Among other things, she and her husband instituted "family night" in the church. "Family night" was simply an open evening, when no church event could be scheduled, for the family to focus on their togetherness as a unit.

Today, all of her children are serving the Lord with joy and grace in a variety of ways in the church. Each is an incredible testimony, not only to their godly parents, but also to the Lord Jesus Christ. The order and joy of their families continue to motivate others to serve the Lord together.

After pastoring for more than forty years, our senior pastor passed on his leadership position to another younger man. It is not surprising that this pastor and his wife are also placing a premium on raising their children. They too make daily, tangible sacrifices to raise them in love and with godly standards. They are such an example to the church that they too are producing fruit that remains in the next generation. This baton is not only worth receiving, but also worth passing on again.

How Can I Keep My Home Stress-Free?

Every set of Christian parents is to raise their children with godliness, motivating them to serve Christ and not provoking them to anger (Ephesians 6:4). However, full-time ministry is the only profession that has as part of its job qualifications an admonition from the Lord Himself to do a good job of parenting. It is as though God builds a glass house, places a leader and his or her family in it and invites people to watch. What pressure!

If you are a leader in the Christian community, no matter what your capacity of involvement, some will criticize you for doing it all wrong, and some will shy away from you because you seem to do it so perfectly. Some will think that you don't give enough time to your children, and some will think that you are overly protective. Some will criticize you for buying your children too many clothes, and some will offer you second hand clothes that are stained and torn in hope of improving their wardrobe. Some will think that you don't give enough time to the church because of your copious dedication to your children, and some will think that you give too much focused time to your children and not enough time to the needs of others.

These are probably enough reasons to tempt you to step out of the spotlight right there! I can honestly tell you that if you look at this pressure from a negative perspective, it will make you an oversensitive, anxious and grumpy parent. Philippians 4:6-7 says, "Be anxious for nothing, but in everything by prayer and supplication, with thanksgiving, let your requests be made known to God; and the peace of God, which surpasses all understanding, will guard your hearts and minds through Christ Jesus."

Look at this opportunity with faith and joy. Being a parent is a privilege and a joy. Being a Christian is a privilege and a joy. Why not allow the two to blend together and become a blessing to many? The key is hidden in this verse, "Imitate me, just as I also imitate Christ" (I Corinthians 11:1). You and your children may stumble a few times, but how you get back up is part of being an example too!

My father was a railroad engineer while I was growing up. There were certain adjustments my mother had to make in her schedule in order to function lovingly with his schedule. As a child, I never remember feeling badly toward my dad for the long hours and weekends he worked. Yet now, as an adult, I realize that my mother made many sacrifices to adjust to his out-of-town schedules and to keep us from noticing his frequent absence.

My dad was involved in my life in so many unique ways that the times when he was not there have been nearly erased from my memory. He worked hard to make up for the unusual work schedule that he had. My mother honored the Lord in her attitude; hence, we as children never felt the pressure of my dad's work schedule. My dad, in turn, sacrificed rest and other hobbies to be involved in our lives, and that made the difference. Attitude and personal involvement go a long way.

I'm saying this to demonstrate that every vocation has its sacrifices. How you convey those sacrifices to your children and how you make up for those sacrifices will determine their attitudes and memories of their childhood. How you approach your schedule will also affect their attitudes toward the Lord and whether serving Him is a privilege or a chore.

How Can I Maintain Flexibility?

In this day and age, work schedules often tend to be different than the typical nine-to-five jobs of a generation ago. If your schedule or your husband's schedule does not follow banker's hours, you can make that work for you in some unique ways. It can be challenging, but it can also be very positive.

As a parent, I chased big wheels up and down the street, coached cookie baking, was the forever taxi and sat at more sporting events than I care to count. My husband was a high school golf coach, basketball coach and personal track coach for our children during their teen years. We were able to do many of these things, not because we weren't busy, but because our schedules were flexible.

If you have evening responsibilities, you and your children may be up late and sleep in on weekends. If you have early morning responsibilities, your family may go to bed early and get up early. Learn to flow with the nature of the vocation and ministry to which God has called you, and let your family do so as well. Allow your children to benefit from the flexibility of your schedule. Make them a significant part of your life by involving them as much as possible. If your ministry is to pray for people at the altar, encourage your children to join you in praying for people if they want to. If your ministry is overseeing the nursery, have your children alongside of you. I realize that this won't work in all areas of ministry, but when it's possible, put it into practice.

If you travel vocationally, occasionally take your children with you as you can afford. My husband and I have sacrificed money and some of our personal desires to allow our children to travel with us at times. Sometimes our trips with our children even cut into their school schedules as well. We had to be flexible with the flexibility given to us.

I am not suggesting that children should not develop study habits or have disciplined school schedules. They should be consistent in their studies and get nutritious meals and regular sleep. That is part of a disciplined life that they need to experience. What I am suggesting is that you should not make your children's schedules rigid when yours is flexible. Let them enjoy the benefits of that flexibility in more ways than one. Let them experience the fulfillment of being discipled and bonding with your generation by working by your side. Enjoy the flexibility the Lord has given you together.

How Can I Face the Challenge of Busyness?

When your work and church involvement is stretched to the maximum, be sensitive to your children. Give them hope by showing them the "light at the end of the tunnel," a special time coming up on the calendar. This is not to say that serving the Lord is a dark tunnel, but the work of it can feel that way to children at times. Their desire to have focused time with you is not overtly selfish but rather is a desire for nurturing.

Children need a rest from busyness from time to time. When parents are overly busy, children need a rest from their parents' schedules. Even if they have been home and tucked in by a loving grandmother every evening, they can feel the busyness of their parents' schedules. They usually don't sleep as peacefully as when they know that their parents' day has ended too. I call this "emotional family bonding." Plainly put, children need the undivided attention of their parents after several busy days and evenings.

This is true not only for small children, but for teens as well. They may not express it, but the need is there. If teens don't receive parental attention on a consistent basis, they may respond in a variety of ways. They may slip into rebellious patterns, such as illicit sex, drug or alcohol abuse, or they may develop eating disorders or associate with friends whose behavior you don't approve. They may quietly withdraw or attempt suicide. Perhaps a less dramatic response, but one with greater parental loss, would be for your children simply to replace your position of influence in their lives with another person. Teens are still in a developmental stage, and they are not always sure how to handle their immature notions with maturity. They need mentors and involved parents. Youth pastors, teachers and coaches can have great influence, but they are not parents to your children. Your teens need you to be there consistently enough that when they need you, they know where to find you. Again, if you aren't there, they may replace you with someone who is there for them. In the busyness of your schedule, this may seem fine with you. However in the long run, this will be a greater loss than you can even begin to imagine.

How Can I Balance Travel and Family Life?

If you and/or your husband travel(s) away from the family, be sensitive to the loss that the children may feel.

As I mentioned in the last chapter, the Lord began to open doors for my husband to travel when our children were still quite young.

When he was away, I worked hard at making it a fun time for our children in special ways. Whether we took special trips to the zoo or just more time at the park, swinging and swimming, we had fun. When we picked up my husband at the airport, as soon as we got inside the car, we would begin to sing a little song about being together again. Then we would stop for a hamburger or ice cream treat, or we would surprise Daddy with cookies at home. He would then begin to tell us the most exciting parts of his journey. It was a memorable and bonding routine. The children missed their daddy. I missed him tearfully at times, but we worked hard at keeping the joy and the purpose of the trip as our focus.

When we both traveled and left the children behind, we always made sure that they were left with families that they enjoyed and we trusted.

As the children got older, my husband phoned regularly, sometimes daily, when he traveled. During these teen years, there was a season during which my husband even submitted his travel schedule to our children to demonstrate their priority in his life. They carried that responsibility very seriously and humbly, and then turned it back over to him after a short period of time. They trusted that he would make the decisions that were best for us as a family and for the Lord.

When our son was in junior high school, he was looking forward to his annual fishing weekend with his dad, when a pastor from across the nation phoned and requested that my husband come for some special meetings in his church. After my husband explained his reason for turning down the request, the pastor offered to provide an airplane ticket and fishing trip for our son if my husband agreed to come. Upon hearing this offer, he presented the opportunity to our son and let him make the choice—the favorite old fishing hole or a new adventure. He chose the new adventure. They had a wonderful weekend, and today our son and his wife are youth pastors in that same church many miles away. Was this just a child's desire for a new adventure, or was it a divine appointment?

Today both of our children love to travel and minister for the Lord. The joy of ministering in different locations is in their hearts and in their spirits. Their vision is tied to the church and beyond, to the uttermost parts of the earth.

Your children can experience this same love and zeal for the calling of the Lord, regardless of your vocation. Providing this experience will cost time and money, but it will be worth it.

How Should I Set Standards for My Children?

All children and teens need to learn and respect standards. Some standards will be family standards, some will be church standards and some will be community standards. If you are going to groom your children to be honorable citizens of your family, your nation and the Kingdom of God, you must set standards in each area and stick to them.

For example, a community standard would be obeying the law and not speeding while driving, even though teens may always want to go fast. A church standard would be tithing, even though it seems more logical to ten-year-olds to buy chocolate bars instead. A family standard might be resting quietly on Sunday afternoons, even though the children would rather go swimming, skiing or skating.

Community standards will vary from state to state and nation to nation, church standards will vary from church to church and family standards will vary from family to family.

When you set standards, be sure to separate your convictions from your desires. Desires can be stretched; they are alterable. Convictions are constant and rarely or never change. For example, you may have a family standard of resting quietly on Sunday afternoons, but by the time your children are teenagers, you may not mind if they spend Sunday afternoons skating, as long as they are back in time for church in the evening. A quiet afternoon would be your desire, whereas going to church would be your conviction.

As a Christian, never put standards on your children only for the sake of your reputation with others. Make sure that the standards you set for them align with the Word of God. This doesn't mean that you have to find a specific scripture for every family standard, but every standard should be backed up by a biblical principle. For example, your standard may be that your teenage daughter should not wear form-fitting, strapless tops. There is no scripture in the Bible that says anything about strapless tops. However, the biblical principle of modesty in I Timothy 2:9 may apply, "In like manner also, that the women adorn themselves in modest apparel . . ."

You also should never put standards on your children that you do not feel are worthwhile standards for other Christian young people. Even though you may not feel strongly enough to suggest them as church standards, you should be able to explain to an older child or teen why you have set the standards for your family.

As a support minister or lay leader in the congregation, you and your family may need to submit to family standards that the senior pastor requires of the leadership team but does not require of the entire church family. You may or may not agree with these standards, but if you are part of the team, you must be willing to yield to these standards. Just as married couples must stand in agreement before their children, though secretly they may disagree and determine to work it out privately, so church staff and lay leadership should abide by the standards that the senior pastor sets in order to demonstrate unity to the congregation. If you feel that the standards aren't reasonable, or the senior pastor isn't willing to discuss them, then you'll have to work on this issue privately with the senior pastor and other members of the leadership team. However, for the sake of the congregation, you must publicly stand together in unity.

How Can I Battle Comparison?

Many children feel pressured to train for the same vocations that their parents have or vocations that their parents want for them. Whether the pressure is self-inflicted or applied by others, children still feel it. This is especially true for children who feel that their parents want them to train for some aspect of the ministry. It is far more valuable when adult children are serving God and doing what they desire voca-tionally, than when adult children become like Eli's sons, shaming their father and God at the gate of the temple. Do your best to make sure that you don't put this pressure on your children.

Tell your children that you want them to hear from God themselves as to what He would have them do with their lives. Let them discern their callings and giftings. If God is not calling them to certain vocations or avenues of service, why should you?

If members of your family from several generations have been in full-time ministry and your children don't feel that full-time ministry is for them, some people will tell them that they're not measuring up to the family precedent. Sometimes, people will shame them in front of others. At other times, people will shower them with false flattery simply because they're members of your family. Somehow, reasoning faculties get crossed, and people think your children are miniature versions of you. Balance the praise and the criticism. Remind your children that they need Jesus and His direction just as much as their friends do, and vice versa. You may even need to remind them that adults need more of Jesus too. Do this carefully so as not to strike a cord of disrespect in them for any adults.

If members of your family from several generations have struggled in their walks with the Lord, your children may also receive unjust repercussions for something that they have never even thought of doing. As much as you may want to protect your children from the expectations that people will put on them, you can't always be there for them in every instance. Your response to unfair expectations and comparisons can either steady your children in the storm or push them away from God and the church. Try to help them understand why people say the things they say. If what has been said is just not worth the explanation, simply embrace them warmly and let God hold their hands and walk them on through bravely.

Don't try to fight the expectations of others or react harshly. Listen carefully, cry softly and pray much. Never forget that God Himself placed your children strategically in your family, not only for your sake and His, but for theirs as well. God is carefully plotting out and planning every step. He is forming and molding them even by the expectations that people put on them. Allow God to deal with them personally–He is a loving Father.

It takes time and energy to deal with those who sincerely care and have a genuine discernment concerning your children, and those who are critical out of selfish motives. Dealing tenderly and logically with your children also takes time–sometimes hours, days and years.

Will The Sacrifices of Parenting Be Worthwhile?

As a contemporary Christian mother and woman who desires to influence her generation for Christ, will your schedule be busy? Will you have to help your children with frustrating science projects, mathematical formulas and youthful, spiritual ups and downs? Will parenting cost time, energy and the development of some of your own personal goals?

Will you experience the thrill of victory and the agony of defeat? Yes, sometimes it will be all of that.

However, you will hardly remember the sacrifices; they will seem but a moment in time. Your today's with children will turn into tomorrow's with grandchildren. Will it be worth the journey? Most definitely!

SECTION FOUR:

*

your
Generation

Chapter 14

WISDOM
A Woman Who Fulfills Her Call

❋

I once heard a story of a little boy who lived in the United States during the Great Depression in the 1930s. He and his family had very little money with which to live.

He made a little boat out of a piece of wood and played with it every day in a nearby stream. It was his only toy. Much to his horror, one day the current captured the boat and carried it away.

Not many days after this, he was walking downtown and noticed his little boat in the window of a second hand store. He went in and said to the storeowner, "That's my boat you have in your window. It's mine. I made it." The store owner replied, "Son, I paid a price for that boat. If you want it back, you'll have to pay for it."

The boy worked for many days, doing every kind of odd job that he could to earn the pennies that it would take to buy back his boat. Finally, he had the required amount. He went back to the store, and there was his boat still in the window.

He excitedly went into the store and purchased it again. He then took it back to the stream to play. As he gently put it into the water, he said to the boat, "I made you, and I paid for you. You're twice owned."

Isn't that what the Master has done for you? He made you, and He paid the price of His Son for you; you are twice His. He has not only redeemed you, but He has also chosen you for a special purpose. Surely He has a purpose for all that He has invested!

I Peter 2:9-10 says, "But you are a chosen generation, a royal priesthood, a holy nation, His own special people, that you may proclaim the praises of Him who called you out of darkness into His marvelous light; who once were not a people but are now the people of God, who had not obtained mercy but now have obtained mercy."

You belong to a people that are scattered throughout the nations. Yet, you belong to the people of God, a generation chosen by Him for His purposes. Regardless of your circumstances, you have a destiny and a responsibility to affect your generation with the strategy and wisdom of God.

How Can I Gain Wisdom?

Wisdom from the Lord must be imparted in order to have a successful strategy for saving this generation. Proverbs chapters one and two say that we each need to know, hear and apply wisdom. Wisdom is key. According to Scripture, wisdom can be found in six places.

In Christ

". . . attaining to all riches of the full assurance of understanding, to the knowledge of the mystery of God, both of the Father and of Christ, in whom are hidden all the treasures of wisdom and knowledge" (Colossians 2:2-3).

"For the message of the cross is foolishness to those who are perishing, but to us who are being saved it is the power of God. . . . Christ the power of God and the wisdom of God. Because the foolishness of

God is wiser than men and the weakness of God is stronger than men" (I Corinthians 1:18-25).

In the Fear of the Lord

"The fear of the Lord is the beginning of wisdom; a good understanding have all those who do His commandments. . . ." (Psalm 111:10).

"For the Lord gives wisdom; from His mouth come knowledge and understanding" (Proverbs 2:6).

"The fear of the Lord is the instruction of wisdom; and before honor is humility" (Proverbs 15:33).

In Sacrificial Living

"I beseech you therefore, brethren, by the mercies of God, that you present your bodies a living sacrifice, holy, acceptable to God, which is your reasonable service" (Romans 12:1).

". . . 'Because this was in your heart, and you have not asked riches or wealth or honor or the life of your enemies, nor have you asked long life—but have asked wisdom and knowledge for yourself, that you may judge My people over whom I have made you king—wisdom and knowledge are granted to you; and I will give you riches and wealth and honor, such as none of the kings have had who were before you, nor shall any after you have the like' " (II Chronicles 1:11-12).

In Asking

" 'Now give me wisdom and knowledge, that I may go out and come in before this people; for who can judge this great people of Yours?' " (II Chronicles 1:10).

"If any of you lack wisdom, let him ask of God, that giveth to all men liberally, and upbraideth not; and it shall be given him" (James 1:5, KJV).

"Only by pride cometh contention: but with the well advised is wisdom" (Proverbs 13:10, KJV).

In Life Experiences

"My brethren, count it all joy when you fall into various trials, knowing that the testing of your faith produces patience. But let patience have its perfect work, that you may be perfect and complete, lacking nothing. If any of you lacks wisdom let him ask of God who gives to all liberally and without reproach, and it will be given to him" (James 1:2-5).

"A wise man fears and departs from evil, but a fool rages and is self-confident" (Proverbs 14:16).

In Reproofs

"A wise son heeds his father's instruction, but a scoffer does not listen to rebuke" (Proverbs 13:1).

"The rod and rebuke give wisdom, but a child left to himself brings shame to his mother" (Proverbs 29:15).

What Is the Fruit of Wisdom?

Wisdom is personified as a woman in the book of Proverbs, but foolishness, the opposite of wisdom, is also exemplified as a woman. This foolish woman is known as "the harlot." These two personifications teach much about wisdom and evil, what to pursue, what to watch out for and what to impart to the next generation. Consider this comparison of the two.

WISDOM

WISDOM	THE HARLOT
Is Obviously Placed	**Stalks in the Dark and Secret Places**
"She takes her stand on the top of the high hill, beside the way, where the paths meet. She cries out by the gates, at the entry of the city, at the entrance of the doors" (Proverbs 8:2-3).	"At times she was outside, at times in the open square, lurking at every corner" (Proverbs 7:12).
Fears the Lord	**Forgets the Covenant of God**
"So that you incline your ear to wisdom . . . then you will understand the fear of the Lord, and find the knowledge of God" (Proverbs 2:2-5).	". . . who forsakes the companion of her youth, and forgets the covenant of her God" (Proverbs 2:17).
Gains Discretion and Discernment	**Delights in Darkness**
"Then you will understand righteousness and justice, equity and every good path. When wisdom enters your heart, and knowledge is pleasant to your soul, discretion will preserve you; understanding will keep you" (Proverbs 2:9-11).	"From those who leave the paths of uprightness to walk in the ways of darkness; who rejoice in doing evil, and delight in the perversity of the wicked; whose ways are crooked, and who are devious in their paths" (Proverbs 2:13-15).
Is Truthful	**Is Dishonest**
"For my mouth will speak truth; wickedness is an abomination to my lips" (Proverbs 8:7).	"With her enticing speech she caused him to yield, with her flattering lips she seduced him" (Proverbs 7:21).
Promises Favor, True Wealth and Longevity	**Promises Nights of Sensual, Devilish Love**
"That I may cause those who love me to inherit wealth . . . for whoever finds me finds life, and obtains favor from the Lord; . . . for by me your days will be multiplied, and years of life will be added to you" (Proverbs 8:21, 35; 9:11).	"Come, let us take our fill of love until morning; let us delight ourselves with love. For my husband is not at home; . . ." (Proverbs 7:18-19).
Brings Life	**Ends in Death**
"For whoever finds me finds life . . . Forsake foolishness and live . . ." (Proverbs 8:35; 9:6).	"For she has cast down many wounded, and all who were slain by her were strong men. Her house is the way to hell, descending to the chambers of death" (Proverbs 7:26-27).

As you can see from this chart, seeking and walking in wisdom bring positive and lasting fruit. Walking away from God with the darkness of the harlot produces death.

What Can I Learn from Esther's Example?

Esther is a wonderful example of a young woman who walked in these principles of wisdom and rescued a generation from the clutches of death. Notice how her life parallels the wisdom of Proverbs.

God Uniquely and Obviously Placed Her

Esther was a young Jewess of the lineage of God's chosen people. However, at this time in history, the Jews had been scattered like seed throughout the nations and were not really considered a nation in their own right. Esther was an orphan, raised by a loving, God-fearing cousin named Mordecai. She grew up in Mordecai's home near the king's court.

The pagan king, Ahasuerus, was in need of a new wife and his servants suggested, ". . . 'Let beautiful young virgins be sought for the king' " (Esther 2:2). Hence, Esther found herself having to leave her comfortable home situation with Mordecai in order for the Lord to strategically place her.

To fully appreciate this, we need to realize that this beauty pageant was not entered into voluntarily. Esther 2:8 says, ". . . Esther also was taken to the king's palace . . ." I don't think that Esther or her beloved cousin would have chosen for her to be considered for this position. What godly, young teen would choose to marry a pagan king who was known for his self-focused drunken celebrations?

Esther lost her parents, and was now separated from her beloved guardian, Mordecai. Where was she to find safety and hope for a future? The prospects were not looking too good. She could either hope to marry a tyrant or be sent away the rest of her days with a group of Persian concubines. That would be enough pressure to cause even a mid-life woman to break out in acne!

After this selection process took place, Esther spent one year in what was considered to be the purification process. She was anointed for six months with oil of myrrh and for six months with perfumes and other preparations and beautification. It was during this year that I believe she was being "purified," not only outwardly, but inwardly as well. With purification and brokenness comes healing and insight.

I am sure that Esther was not excited about the prospects of being married to an ungodly despot or joining his harem. She must have experienced disappointment that could have led to depression if she chose to allow it.

During this year of anointing, Esther must have called out to God numerous times for His encouragement and wisdom. After all, what could she offer to this grand beauty pageant that other girls could not? Queen Vashti had been noted throughout the known world for her beauty. What could a humble young Jewess have to offer in light of a beautiful Persian woman for whom the king's heart still longed? Only the beauty of holiness and the wisdom of God could outshine the rest.

She Feared the Lord

Esther feared the Lord. She feared God more than she cared for her own life. It was this reverence that made her willing to sacrifice herself in the hour of need. The proof of this fear of God is found in her refusal to be pressured by the circumstances at hand. When her cousin told her of the plight of their people and requested that she expose her heritage and plead on their behalf, she determined to spend three days in prayer and fasting first. She refused to be pressured by the circumstances of time. She was willing to wait on God and to move with the knowledge of His forethought in order to accomplish His purpose.

The Persian law, at this time, held that one of royal lineage could only marry a woman who belonged to one of the seven great Persian families. Therefore, the marriage of Ahasuerus to Esther, a Jewess, was actually against Persian law. For Esther to reveal her heritage took great courage and wisdom. She needed good timing for such a disclosure, to be sure.

In chapter four and verse eight, when Mordecai sent a command to Esther to go in to the king and make supplication for their people, Esther first responded, "Oh no!" By the time she, her maids and all the Jews had fasted for three days, her "Oh no!" transformed into, "I know! I know what I will do; the strategy of the Lord has come to me." As she waited on the Lord and feared Him first, her fear of man subsided, and the Lord's strategy came to her. She knew what to do to win the heart of the king, even at the risk of exposing her own lineage.

She Moved with Discretion and Discernment

Next, in this story of intrigue, we see that Esther moved with discretion and discernment. It was a serious breach of protocol for anyone to enter the king's inner court without being summoned. It could mean a death sentence unless he chose to raise his scepter of acceptance and allow entrance. Queen Vashti had not previously broken protocol; she had merely refused the king's drunken desire and was banished from the kingdom. For Esther to make this attempt was risky, at best, and possibly deadly.

This king and his men had ridded themselves of one out-of-order queen; they certainly could do it again. There were many beautiful women waiting in the wings to have an opportunity to be queen. Esther was indispensable to God and to her people, but not to king Ahasuerus and his men. Vashti had been beautiful, but not wise. Esther was both beautiful and wise. The anointing oil massaged into her spirit gave her not only strength to rescue a nation, but softness to woo the heart of a king.

When Esther's "Oh no" was transformed into "I know," she rose up and put on her royal robes. She stood in the inner court of the king's palace and waited for him to allow her entrance. She came with a strategy of war in her heart that would bring peace to the kingdom. It is interesting to note that Esther did not rise up to make her move until the third day of her fast. Christ also arose on the third day, stood in the midst of his disciples and said, ". . . Peace be with you." He also came with a strategy for war that would bring peace to the Kingdom.

Esther invited her husband, Ahasuerus, and her enemy, Prince Haman, to dinner. She must have known the king's personality, favorite food and atmosphere. I believe that Esther had studied this man. She knew how to discern his moods and his desires. She knew what would provoke the most positive response in him.

She was not hasty in making her request known, but moved with discretion and discernment. While she waited between dinner engagements, the prince of deception foolishly arranged his own demise. He built a gallows on which to hang godly Mordecai. Little did he realize that he was dealing with a woman of strategy and wisdom.

At this same interlude, the king was unable to sleep and had the chronicles of his reign read to lull him to sleep. As he listened, the whispers of intercession covered his mind, unbeknownst to him. He heard not only annals, but also the name of Mordecai, a man who had saved his life and was yet unrewarded. Before going to sleep, he decided to have Prince Haman bring honor to Mordecai the following day.

As Prince Haman lead the escort team to honor Mordecai, his nerves began to tighten and unravel. After the grand parade, Haman hastened to Queen Esther's banquet feast.

She Spoke the Simple Truth

Esther had the feast prepared, served the king and his prince, and waited for the question to come. When the king asked, ". . . 'What is your petition, Queen Esther? It shall be granted you. And what is your request, up to half the kingdom? It shall be done!' " Esther spoke the simple truth (Esther 7:2). She didn't waste any words, as some women with lesser wisdom would. She spoke of concern for herself, whom he loved, and for her people, whom he did not know. She then quickly moved on and spoke of concern for the king and his reputation. She waited for the responsive question and very simply spoke the truth with two pointed words, "enemy" and "wicked." She made her point honestly and simply. What a Holy Spirit led strategy!

Later, she came again in humility, with simple truth in her words, and made petition for her people in regard to Haman's decree (Esther 8).

She Attained Favor and Longevity for Her People

The result of Esther's wise deeds was that she attained favor and longevity for her people. She brought life to herself and to her people. Her strategy for war was birthed out of her willingness to be placed by God. It came through the avenue of reverence, discretion, discernment and truth. She was the quintessential instrument of the spirit of wisdom, and she rescued a generation.

You too are called to be a rescuer of a generation. You too are called to move in wisdom. Isaiah 43:1 says, ". . . 'Fear not, for I have redeemed you; I have called you by your name; You are Mine.' "

What Is to Be My Strategy for Saving a Generation?

I would like to include here a simple strategy for rescuing this generation. It is actually a very basic safety formula that your parents probably taught you as a child: stop, look, listen and proceed.

Stop

In Isaiah chapter six, Isaiah was in the midst of a stressful time in his life. King Uzziah, a beloved king to Isaiah, had just died. King Amaziah, the previous ruler, had been a wicked king. Uzziah had been a good king, of whom Scripture says, "And he did what was right in the sight of the Lord . . ." (II Chronicles 26:4). He became king when he was just sixteen years old and reigned for fifty-two years in Jerusalem.

Toward the end of his reign, he let pride get in his way and went in to burn incense to the Lord. Only the priests were allowed to do this, and when the priests withstood him, he got angry. In the middle of his rage, leprosy broke out on his forehead. He was leprous until he died at the age of sixty-eight. It's in this context that we come to Isaiah in chapter six. I don't believe that he was just chronicling time for us. I believe that he was letting the reader know that, even in times of stress and sadness, the call of the Lord can come if you will but posture yourself to receive.

Stress will come. Times of sadness, as well as joy, will come. In the midst of all the busyness and disappointments that come your way, stop in God's presence. Isaiah 40:31 says, "But those who wait on the Lord shall renew their strength; they shall mount up with wings like eagles, they shall run and not be weary, they shall walk and not faint."

Church historians tell us that the apostle John once said, "The bow that is always bent will cease to shoot straight." In other words, there will be times when you need to stop, even for the sake of the people you want to reach for the Lord. You must not let the busyness of life prevent you from stopping in His presence. For it is in His presence that you will receive renewed strength and fresh perspective. So stop.

Look

In verse one of Isaiah six, Isaiah said, ". . . I saw the Lord . . ." Then he went on to describe all that he saw of the Lord and His throne room. In the midst of this glorious vision, he suddenly saw himself and proclaimed in verse five, ". . . 'Woe is me, for I am undone!' "

As he confessed what he saw in himself in the presence of the King, a seraphim swooped down, touched his mouth with a live coal from the altar and removed his iniquity. Now that's some angelic lip service!

"Touched" in this passage means "atoned for." James 3:6 says, "And the tongue is a fire, a world of iniquity. . . ." It needs a touch from a live coal from the altar of God. It needs atonement. Cry out to Him in humility, and let Him touch your speech with His redeeming fire. His redemption paid the price to anoint your speech.

Stop in His presence and look. Look into His Word, into His presence, until you can see clearly who He is and who you are. Then humble yourself before Him in acknowledgement of your need for His atoning grace. The result will be an anointed tongue.

Listen

In the midst of Isaiah's unparalleled vision of the holiness of God, contrasted with his own sinfulness, and the anointing of fire that was placed on his tongue, he heard the voice of the Lord. In fact, he tuned into a conversation going on between the Godhead. They were saying in verse eight, ". . . 'Whom shall I send, and who will go for us?' " Isaiah was not only lit on fire by the presence of the Lord, but he was also tuned in to His voice.

You also will need to be tuned in to the voice of the Father to walk in His anointing. People are counting on you not to speak out of your own perspective alone. Rather, they need to hear the perspective and strategy of the Lord. They will not hear if you will not listen. As a Christian woman walking in the calling and anointing of God, you must cease from your busyness at times, and just listen.

Yes, people will sometimes get upset with you for not always being there for them. But they will be more upset if your influence doesn't accurately represent the voice and nature of God. This, of course, is not meant to take away from the importance of hearing from God individually. This is only to say that people will depend on you in surprising ways, simply because you are a woman who is determined to walk in God's calling and anointing.

Isaiah had to prophesy to a people. You have to influence a people. Your listening skills will affect your strategy for bringing in and keeping the harvest. You must stop, look and listen. This is a requirement of the call.

Proceed

After tuning in on the heavenly conversation, Isaiah could hardly contain himself. He cried out, "Hear am I! Send me." It's not good enough to simply stop, look and listen. You must be willing to go. Proceed with caution, yes; but do proceed. There is a harvest worth harvesting.

Isaiah had a hard message to give to the people of his day. At the end of the message, the Lord told him ever so carefully, " '. . . the holy seed shall be its stump' " (Isaiah 6:13). When you look to the fields, look carefully. It may seem that the fields have been burned over, but look again. There is a "holy seed" within the stump.

In New Testament times, the Samaritans commonly wore white. In John chapter four, after Jesus met with the woman at the well, she left her water pot and went into her city to bring her people out to the well to meet the Master. She left all that represented her shame and her lifestyle–she left her water pot in the heat of the day.

While she was away, the disciples returned with lunch, and Jesus told them that He was not hungry. They were confused and he explained that His food was ". . . to do the will of Him who sent Me . . ." They probably noticed the water pot and wondered what unclean Samaritan had been feeding Him while they were away. Then He challenged their Jewish pride to ". . . look at the fields, for they are already white for harvest!" (John 4:35). The Samaritans were coming over the fields to meet the Master.

The Master will ask you to lay down every prejudice in order to see the need of the harvest clearly. Truly there is "holy seed" within the stump; and the fields are full. "The mystery which has been hidden from ages and from generations, but now has been revealed to His saints. To them God willed to make known what are the riches of the glory of this mystery among the Gentiles: which is Christ in you, the hope of glory" (Colossians 1:26-27). Christ in you and Christ in them is the hope of glory. Stop and think about it.

Let the Lord's message burn brightly within your heart. Fear not to seek a strategy and receive wisdom from the Lord. It's yours for the asking. There is a harvest waiting to be reaped. You are needed in the field. Stop. Look. Listen. Proceed.

What is My Part in the Harvest?

In chapter one I challenged you with the thought, "God has anointed you–now deal with it." You are anointed. You are needed.

Ephesians 4:14-16 says, ". . . we should no longer be children, tossed to and fro and carried about with every wind of doctrine, by the trickery of men, in the cunning craftiness of deceitful plotting, but, speaking the truth in love, may grow up in all things into Him who is the head-Christ-from whom the whole body, joined and knit together by what every joint supplies, according to the effective working by which every part does its share, causes growth of the body for the edifying of itself in love."

Each member, male or female, married or single, degreed or illiterate, rich or poor, is needed to be a functioning member of the Body of Christ. I pray that at some time in your reading, you stopped and said, "I could do that," "I'm good at that," or "I could be a harvester in that area." I hope that you recognized an anointing from the Lord in different areas mentioned. As Jesus said so clearly, in the books of Matthew and Luke, the harvest is so great and the laborers are so few.

If you have let your talents and gifts sit on the shelf for a while now, dust them off, pick them back up and go again. As Mary said to the servants at the wedding feast, ". . . 'Whatever He says to you, do it' " (John 2:5). A wedding is about to take place, and the servants of the Lord need to busy themselves, doing whatever He tells them to do. Take your talents back to your prayer closet, and see what fresh anointing oil He will pour on them. We are going to war to rescue a generation and bring people to the great wedding feast.

In Jesus' day, soldiers had leather shields to carry into battle. Before entering the battlefield, they spent time massaging fresh oil into the leather to soften it. They did this so that the shield could withstand the blows of the enemy and would not crack easily while under attack. The calling of the Lord does not exempt you from attack. God never promises that this life will be easy, but He does promise to be with us. Psalm 32:8 says, "I will instruct you and guide you along the best pathway for your life; I will advise you and watch your progress" (Living).

Enter His presence daily, and let His anointing oil pour over you afresh, for the harvest is ripe. He has need of you. He is longing to rescue a generation, but the rescue will not take place without every member doing his or her part. Join in on the fun!

Woman you are Called & Anointed.
Cry out, "Here Am I! Send me."

Also Available Through City Bible Publishing

Seasons of Intercession
Frank Damazio

Seasons of Intercession is a progressive journey on which readers will learn the necessity for intercessory prayer that will change their lives, empower churches and shape their futures.
ISBN 1-886849-08-0

Seasons of Revival
Frank Damazio

Seasons of Revival offers fresh insight in understanding God's seasons of outpouring. The truths presented will enable you to enjoy greater refreshing during this season of revival.
ISBN 1-886849-04-8

Covenants
Kevin Conner & Ken Malmin

Covenants gives a biblical framework for understanding the administration of God's dealings with mankind throughout human history.
ISBN 0-914936-77-8

Interpreting the Symbols and Types
Kevin Conner

Interpreting the Symbols and Types is a comprehensive study unlocking the biblical language of the symbol and type, allowing for a greater understanding of scriptural truth.
ISBN 0-914936-51-4

Old Testament Survey New Testament Survey
Kevin Conner & Ken Malmin

These two books address the New Testament and the Old Testament in succinct understandable points. They are designed to give a patterned glimpse of each book of the Bible.
OTS ISBN 0-914936-21-2
NTS ISBN 0-914936-22-0

The Making of a Leader
Frank Damazio

This bestseller presents a scriptural analysis of the philosophy, history, qualifications and practice of Christian leadership. You will be challenged by the illustrations from the life of David and others.
ISBN 0-914936-84-0

Ask for these resources at your local Christian bookstore.

City Bible Publishing is a ministry of
City Bible Church in Portland, Oregon.
Call 1-800-777-6057 for a complete catalog.